WRITERS AND THEIR WORK

ISOBEL ARMSTRONG
General Editor

T0324223

BRAM STOKER

A FILIAL REPROOF.

Mamma (to Noel, who is inclined to be talkative). "HUSH, NOEL! HAVEN'T I TOLD YOU OFTEN THAT LITTLE BOYS SHOULD BE *SEEN* AND NOT *HEARD*?" *Noel.* "YES, MAMMA! BUT YOU DON'T *LOOK AT ME!*"

A cartoon of Bram Stoker and his family by George Du Maurier, from *Punch* 1886.

BRAM STOKER

Andrew Maunder

NORTHCOTE

BRITISH
COUNCIL

© Copyright 2006 by Andrew Maunder

First published in 2006 by Northcote House Publishers Ltd, Horndon, Tavistock, Devon, PL19 9NQ, United Kingdom.
Tel: +44 (0) 1822 810066 Fax: +44 (0) 1822 810034.

British Library Cataloguing-in-Publication Data
A catalogue record for this book is available from the British Library

ISBN 0-7463-1102-8 hardcover
    0-7463-0968-6 paperback

Typeset by PDQ Typesetting, Newcastle-under-Lyme
Printed and bound in the United Kingdom
by Athenaeum Press Ltd., Gateshead, Tyne & Wear

Contents

Acknowledgements

My thanks to Isobel Armstrong and Brian Hulme, and to Simon Avery, William Hughes, Mark Knight, Graham Law, Emma Liggins, Lillian Nayder, Wanda Opalinska, and Anita Pacheco.

This book is dedicated to Liz and Brian Maunder.

Biographical Outline

* Indicates short story collection

1847   8 November, born Abraham Stoker at 15, The Crescent, Clontarf, County Dublin, the third child of Abraham Stoker, a Protestant, Civil Service clerk, and his wife Charlotte Blake Thornley. His early childhood is spent as an invalid. He is close to his brothers, Thornley and George, both of whom become doctors.

1859   Attends the Reverend William Wood's private day school in Dublin (until 1863).

1864   (November): enters Trinity College, Dublin, where he studies science and mathematics. He becomes a prize-winning athlete, standing six feet 2 inches tall, weighing 175 pounds, excelling at rugby, running, rowing, swimming and weightlifting. Serves as President of the Philosophical Society. Delivers his first speech on 'Sensationalism in Fiction and Society'.

1867   Serves as President of the Philosophical Society. In August, he attends a touring production of *The Rivals* at the Theatre Royal Dublin and sees Henry Irving in the role of Jack Absolute.

1870   1 May: awarded BA. Enters the Civil Service at Dublin Castle as a clerk of the Petty Sessions.

1871   November: begins five-year period as theatre reviewer for the *Dublin Evening Mail*. Forms platonic friendships with two actresses, Helen Barry and Genevieve Ward.

1872   Abraham Stoker (senior), now retired, moves with his wife and daughters to Clarens, Switzerland, where they can live more cheaply. Stoker begins an admiring correspondence with the American poet Walt Whitman, whose homoerotic verse was controversial. His short story, 'The Crystal Cup' is published in *London Society*. 'Jack Harmon's Vote' is rejected by *Blackwood's Magazine*. Begins to become a familiar figure in Dublin cultural society and visits the home of Sir William and Lady Wilde and their son, Oscar, in Merrion Square.

1873   Made Editor of the new evening periodical the *Irish Echo* (November).

1874   Resigns as Editor of the *Echo*.

1875   A five-part serial 'The Primrose Path', and two novellas *Buried Treasures* and *The Chain of Destiny* published in *The Shamrock*.

1876   His father dies (October). In December, Stoker sees Irving as Hamlet at the Theatre Royal, Dublin. He writes a flattering review of the actor's performance and is invited to dinner by Irving. The actor's recitation of 'The Dream of Eugene Aram' causes Stoker to collapse into hysterics. Irving is impressed by Stoker's devotion and the two men strike up a friendship.

1877   Promoted to the post of Inspector of Petty Sessions and he travels round Ireland with the magistrate's court.

1878   November: Irving summons Stoker to Glasgow and invites him to take up the post of business manager at the Lyceum Theatre, London. Irving also recruits the actress, Ellen Terry to the Lyceum company; she and Stoker become close friends. On the 4 December, Stoker marries 20-year old society beauty, Florence Anne Lemon Balcombe. The couple move immediately to London and settle at 7, Southampton Street, Covent Garden. Stoker throws himself into his new work.

1879   31 December: Florence gives birth to a son, Noel. He is the couple's only child. Stoker's reference manual, based on his experience of this position, *Duties of the Clerks of the Petty Sessions* is published.

1880   'The Spectre of Doom' published in the *Dublin Evening Mail* (November).

1881   The Stokers, now well known in London society, move to 27 Cheyne Walk, Chelsea.

1882   Stoker receives a bronze medal from the Humane

	Society for his attempted rescue of a drowning man in the Thames. *Under the Sunset** published. Moves to 17 St Leonard's Terrace, Chelsea.
1883	Stoker accompanies the Lyceum company on a tour of North America (October). There are further trips in 1885, 1887 and 1899.
1884	March: Stoker finally meets Walt Whitman.
1885	Delivers an admiring lecture 'A Glimpse of America' at the London Institution (it is published the following year). His only published poem 'One Thing Needful', appears in the American magazine *Youth's Companion*.
1886	'Our New House' published in *The Theatre Annual* (December).
1887	Stoker goes on a third North American tour. 'The Dualitists' published in *The Theatre Annual* (December).
1888	'Death in the Wings' published in Collier's Magazine (November).
1890	Stoker decides to become a barrister and is called to the Bar of the Inner Temple but he never practices law (April). *The Snake's Pass* begins serialisation in *The People* and is syndicated to the *Cardiff Weekly Mail* (July). Begins research for Dracula whilst on holiday in Whitby (August).
1891	Collaborates with 23 well-known novelists on *The Fate of Fenella*, serialised in *The Gentlewoman* (November 1891–May 1892). The novel is published in its entirety in June 1892. 'The Judge's House' published in *Holly Leaves* (December). With the publisher William Heinemann, he sets up The English Library, a venture designed to produce cheap European editions of popular authors. It is short-lived.
1892	'The Secret of the Growing Gold' published in *Black and White* (January).
1893	'The Squaw' published in the *Illustrated Sporting and Dramatic News* (December).
1894	'The Man from Shorrox' published, *Pall Mall Magazine* (February). 'The Red Stockade' published in *Cosmopolitan Magazine*. 'Crooken Sands' published in the *Illustrated Sporting and Dramatic News* (December). 'A Dream of Read Hands' published in *The Sketch*. (September).

1895   *The Watter's Mou* and *The Shoulder of Shasta* published. Irving is knighted by Queen Victoria, as is Stoker's brother Thornley, President of the Royal College of Surgeons.

1896   The Stokers move next door to 18 St Leonard's Terrace, Chelsea.

1897   *Dracula* published (May). Stoker hopes to have the novel performed on stage and organises a copyright reading at the Lyceum. Irving judges the work 'dreadful'.

1898   *Miss Betty* published (February). A dramatised reading takes place on 31 January.

1899   Stoker edits *Sir Henry Irving and Miss Ellen Terry in 'Robespierre', 'The Merchant of Venice', 'The Bells', 'Nance Oldfield', 'The Amber Heart', 'Waterloo', etc.*, a series of etchings of Irving and Terry in performance. Stoker accompanies the Lyceum company on another tour of North America.

1900   Irving faces bankruptcy and signs the Lyceum over to a syndicate.

1901   Death of Oscar Wilde in Paris.

1902   *The Mystery of the Sea* published. Charlotte Stoker dies. The Lyceum company collapses. It closes on 19 July, after a gala celebrating the coronation of King Edward VII. Stoker turns to writing full-time.

1903   *The Jewel of Seven Stars* published. 'A Criminal Star' published (October). Stoker accompanies Irving on a tour of North America.

1904   Florence Stoker converts to Roman Catholicism.

1905   *The Man* published. On 13 October, Henry Irving dies whilst on tour and is buried in Westminster Abbey.

1906   Stoker publishes *Personal Reminiscences of Henry Irving*. It is one of his most successful books. He suffers a paralytic stroke, which leaves him bed-ridden for some months. He remains in poor health for the rest of his life.

1907   Moves to smaller flat at 4 Durham Place, Chelsea. Serves on the staff of the *Daily Telegraph*. Publishes a series of interviews with eminent men of the day – Winston Churchill, W. S. Gilbert, Arthur W. Pinero – for the New York *World*. Addresses the Author's Club on 'The Censorship of Fiction' (November). The talk (later published as an article in *Nineteenth Century* (1908) causes controversy for its outspoken, conservative stance. Writes a companion piece, 'The Censorship of Stage Plays'.

1908   Stoker obtains a post as organiser of the 1908 Paris Theatrical Exhibition. *Lady Athlyne* published. 'The 'Eroes of the Thames' published in the *Royal Magazine* (October). *Snowbound: The Record of a Theatrical Touring Party** published.

1909   Stoker suffers a second stroke. 'The Way of Peace' published in *Everybody's Story Magazine* (December).

1910   Stoker has a second stroke. *Famous Impostors* published.

1911   Financial difficulties force another move to 26 George Square, Belgravia. Stoker applies to the Royal Literary Fund for a grant and, supported by W. S. Gilbert and Anne Thackeray, is awarded £100. *The Lair of the White Worm* published.

1912   20 April: Stoker dies, aged 64. The death certificate records a verdict of 'exhaustion'. Stoker leaves his estate, valued at £4,664, to his wife. He is cremated at Golders Green Cemetery, London.

1914   Florence Stoker arranges the publication of *Dracula's Guest and other Weird Stories*. The patriotic short story, 'Greater Love' published in *The London Magazine*.

1922   First film based on *Dracula*, *Nosferatu* is released in Germany. Florence Stoker petitions to have it destroyed.

1937   Florence Stoker dies, aged 91.

Abbreviations

Introduction

On 24 April 1912, about twenty people gathered in the crypt of Golders Green Cemetery, the extensive Victorian burial ground that fills a large part of the North London suburb. They had come to witness the interment of Bram Stoker, novelist, journalist, theatre manager, who had, as *The Times* noted, 'managed to find time, amid much arduous and distracting work to write a good deal' and, in doing so, to have become 'the master of a particularly lurid and creepy kind of fiction'.[1] Amongst those paying their respects were Stoker's wife, Florence, his only son, Noel, and a small collection of some of the most distinguished people of the day: the novelists Mary Braddon and Ford Madox Ford, the dramatist Arthur Wing Pinero, and the actress Ellen Terry, her son, Gordon Craig, and Laurence Irving (the son of Stoker's late employer, the legendary actor-manager Henry Irving). The tributes were led by the popular novelist Hall Caine, who recalled Stoker's 'massive and muscular and almost volcanic personality that must have been familiar by sight to many thousands in Great Britain and America.' But Caine also expressed the thoughts of many when he suggested that if Stoker were remembered at all (which seemed unlikely) it would be solely for his intense relationship with Henry Irving, which comprised 'his whole life', rather than for any important literary endeavours. In any case, as Caine explained, somewhat patronizingly, Stoker 'had no love of the limelight', being 'fully conscious that he had not other claims to greatness.'[2] He would not expect or want anything more.

Were they around today, Stoker's mourners would no doubt be surprised at the interest that Bram Stoker generates. Prompted largely by *Dracula*, claims for Stoker's 'greatness'

1

have appeared in a multitude of settings. He is read, taught and studied throughout the world, and his presence felt in many different locations. To log on to that part of the World Wide Web containing 'Dracula's Castle' or the Dracula Society is to realise quickly that the activity of reading this Victorian-Edwardian novelist is not confined to the classroom. Indeed, as the words that greet visitors to these disembodied sites suggest, these are spaces that welcome lone travellers, inviting them to 'come freely, go safely'.[3] This multitude of sites is also a reminder that like a handful of other 'classic' authors – William Shakespeare, Jane Austen, Oscar Wilde – Stoker is not the exclusive property of academe, that he has his feet in a number of different camps: 'high' and 'low' culture, the university, the tabloid newspaper, the broadsheet, and the video store.

The discussions that occupy visitors to the cyberspace version of Dracula's castle (and its assorted chatrooms) reveal that there is plenty to talk about. Amongst the growing number of Stoker's novels and short stories in print, there are over a hundred editions of *Dracula* – including numerous abridged and illustrated versions for children. Add to this the many interpretations of Stoker's work offered by recent film and theatre adaptations: Ken Russell's camp *The Lair of the White Worm* (1988), Francis Ford Coppola's lavish *Bram Stoker's 'Dracula'* (1992), Northern Ballet Theatre's celebrated touring production of *Dracula* (1996), Jonathan Holloway's theatrical adaptation of the same novel, *Nosferatu: The Visitor*, set in post-Holocaust London (2000), E. Elias Merhige's *Shadow of the Vampire* (2001), a dramatization of the strange goings-on that accompanied the making of another film about Dracula, the 1922 German silent classic *Nosferatu – Eine Symphonie des Grauens (Nosferatu – A Symphony of Horror)*, Wes Craven's updated *Dracula: 2001* and Joerg Witzch's *Count Dracula: The Musical* (2001).[4] Fans can also debate the novelist Tom Holland's fictional representation of a certain Bram Stoker 'detective' who appears 'as himself', alongside Oscar Wilde and (bizarrely) Lord Byron in the gothic, Jack-the-Ripper London of the 1880s in *Supping with Panthers* (1996). Then there is the American actress Peta Wilson's turn as a post-Dracula Mina Harker (complete with bite marks) in the high-tech blockbuster *The League of Extraordinary Gentlemen* (2003). Based on Alan Moore's best-selling series of comic books about the adventures of a team of Victorian superheroes recruited to save the world – Alan Quatermain (Sean Connery), Captain Nemo (Naseeruddin Shah), secret service agent Tom Sawyer (Shane West), Dorian Gray (Stuart Townsend), and Dr. Jekyll/Mr. Hyde (Jason Flemyng) – the reappearance in this group of Stoker's most famous heroine, and the sole woman, is further testimony to a desire to keep the novelist and his characters alive and talking.

Nor is this the only guise in which Stoker has recently emerged. It is not difficult to forget the hilarity stoked up by the British media in 1997 when the British Home Office minister Ann Widdecombe (in the unlikely guise of Mina Harker) spoke of her boss, the Home Secretary, Michael Howard, as having 'something of the night about him'.[5] Few needed to have the allusion explained to them.[6] 1997 was (as *The Independent* noted) Stoker's year, prompting 'a slew of Dracula-related items'.[7] *The Times* reported that attempts by Dracula enthusiasts to mark the centenary with a march on Whitby Cathedral had been opposed by church authorities as 'un-christian'.[8] Under the heading 'World News' the same paper reported the Romanian military's decision to name its new combat helicopter the AH1 RO–Dracula after the Transylvanian bloodsucker; this expansive move was seen as Romania's desire to be in the first wave of NATO enlargement.[9] Stoker has also taken his place on the Irish Tourist Board's list of potential visitor attractions; in 1997 the Irish Post Office issued a set of commemorative stamps to mark the 150th anniversary of his birth. More recently, in 2001 the *Evening Standard* gave the headline 'Waugh's Count Draculas bloodied but unbeatable' to an article about the victorious touring Australian cricket team captained by Steve Waugh, a member of whom had had his face gashed by a can of lager thrown from a hostile Lords crowd; reporter Ian Chadband predicted of the Australian team that 'after scenting blood these past weeks they are ready to tuck into the main course with relish at Edgbaston a week on Thursday'.[10] In thinking about Stoker's contemporary reception we might also note, too, the specialist clothing shops set up to meet the needs of those who fantasize about being Count Dracula. Then there is the mass-appeal of Anne Rice's Stoker-infected Lestat chronicles, and even *Buffy the Vampire Slayer*, a television series which is to

3

Dracula what the films *Clueless* (1995) and *O* (2001) were to Jane Austen's *Emma* and Shakespeare's *Othello* – literary classics given a glamorous teenage makeover.

For the past decade, it has been increasingly difficult to close our eyes and ears to the exploitation of Bram Stoker and his characters. This includes the lazy invocation of them when anything sinister or untoward takes place. Amongst all this, however, a definite pattern has emerged. The recent splurge of vampire mania on the part of Hollywood studios and the success of re-writes like Kim Newman's *Dracula Cha Cha Cha* (2001) and Christopher Schildt's *House of Dracula* (2001) – the latter billed as the story of 'a mysterious stranger who stalks the gleaming cities and urban landscapes of the twenty-first century' – clearly has much to do with the much-touted belief that Stoker's stories, notably *Dracula*, manifest certain 'timeless truths', that everyone can recognize, plus of course a sense that, in terms of revenue, there are profits to be had in blood-sucking.[11] There is also a sense in the case of *Dracula*, that this novel is infinitely adaptable and accommodating, exerting a hypnotic fascination, 'persisting across cultures and times' as the *New York Times* recently put it.[12] In 2002, leading articles in the British press reported the guilty verdict passed on a teenager who (seemingly obsessed with vampires) had brutally mur-dered and dismembered a 90-year old pensioner, believing that he could gain immortality by drinking her blood. The same reports dutifully recorded how when he was arrested, the teenager repeatedly said 'Bite my neck', and noted too how amongst his possessions was a well-thumbed copy of *Dracula*.[13] It is perhaps a sign of the times as well that when, in 1998, *The Guardian* ran a feature on Universal Pictures' action-adventure film *The Mummy*, starring Brendan Fraser and Rachel Weisz, one of the sources to be called up by reporter Jonathan Jones was Stoker's 'erotic' novel *The Jewel of Seven Stars* (1903). What was flagged up, however, was not just Stoker's ability to tell an exciting story but the modern resonance of the 'father-daughter incest' theme and his ability to 'go beyond imperial theatrics to explore a disturbing territory where the Western moral order disintegrates'.[14]

I list these examples because one of the issues I want to consider in this study is Stoker's reception history and his meaning for different generations of readers. It is clearly significant that one section of current critical opinion presents Stoker's works as very much 'of their time' (i.e. the 1890s and 1900s), whilst another section finds in them the 'potential to speak to the anxieties [and] desires of the twentieth [and twenty-first] century'.[15] 'The most subtle mirror of our desires and discontent' was how Eric Korn described Count Dracula in a 1995 article appearing in that august publication the *Times Literary Supplement*.[16,17] Such reports seem to support Nina Auerbach's claim that Stoker's most famous character 'symbolizes our evil and impersonal age' and 'reflect[s] our culture's ethical debates'.[18]

But are his characters really mirrors of 'ourselves'?[19] How does Stoker belong to us? What do Stoker's novels mean to us? Answers to this question fluctuate wildly. There is Stoker the producer of hastily-written sadistic shockers, 'flighty malarkey about sexed-up vampires and imaginary worlds', as Ed Power puts it, whose novels are the provenance of 'anoraks', grave-spotters and '*Star Trek*-besotted square pegs'.[20] There is another Stoker – Stoker the reactionary, whose novels articulate bigoted fears – fears of women, of sexual dislocation, of homosexuality disguised as homosociality, of disease, of the collapse of empires, of invasion, and of the past. Then there is Stoker the prophet who deals in universal, timeless issues, 'fundamental human stuff that everyone feels and knows', as the film director Francis Ford Coppola announced when explaining the vision behind his own (re)interpretation of *Bram Stoker's 'Dracula'* in 1992.[21] It is this Stoker, for example, who prompts the theories that the new millennium and HIV both explain the penchant for vampirism. Whatever one's take on him, what is certainly true is that these different views of Stoker – both man and novelist – set the terms for a critical debate that is still being played out and is certainly set to continue.

WHO WAS BRAM STOKER?

Who was this man whose work provokes such interest? One response is that, despite a great deal of detailed biographical attention, Bram Stoker remains a fairly indeterminate and often obscured figure, so much so that it is usual to preface biographical accounts of his life with the proviso that he is an 'enigma'.

What, then, do we actually know about him? He was born Abraham Stoker into a modest Irish-Protestant family at Clontarf, Dublin, on 8 November 1847. His father, also called Abraham, was a respectable civil servant for the British government at Dublin Castle, and his mother Charlotte was active in charity work among the working classes. By accounts he was an ailing child, confined to bed and unable to walk until the age of seven. However, by 1864, he seems to have recovered sufficiently to enter Trinity College, Dublin, as a student of science and mathematics. The sickly Abraham had transmogrified into the strapping 'Bram', a prizewinning athlete, standing six feet 2 inches tall, weighing 175 pounds, excelling at rugby, running, rowing, swimming and weightlifting. This image of a 'hearty', masculine, sportsman, was one that held for over forty years (bolstered by a much publicized incident in 1882 when he leapt into the Thames in an attempt to save a drowning man). 'The embodiment of health and strength and geniality' was how the *New York Times* described him.[22] For the *British Weekly* he was 'cordial', 'faithful' and above all 'chivalrous'.[23] Through Stoker's own words we can glimpse him: 'ugly but strong and determined...a large bump over my eyebrows...a heavy jaw and a big mouth and thick lips – sensitive nostrils – a snub nose and straight hair...equal in temper and cool in disposition...'.[24]

When, in 1870, Stoker graduated with a BA in mathematics, he dutifully followed his father into the Civil Service, assuming the position of Clerk to the Registrar of Petty Sessions, where he worked for the next eight years. In the evenings he took on another literary role, that of (unpaid) drama critic of the *Dublin Evening Mail*. It was in this capacity that his career took an unexpected direction when, in 1876, he had his first emotional meeting with the man who would to all intents and purposes become his life partner, the actor Henry Irving (1835–1905). 'Soul had looked into soul!' Stoker later claimed. 'From that hour began a friendship as profound, as close, as lasting as can be between two men...the sight of his picture before me with those loving words...unmans me once again as I write' (*PR* I 33).

Irving, charismatic and immensely egotistical, looked for idolatrous hero-worship and in Stoker, a man who had a tendency to form passionate attachments to dynamic, older, creative men (there had been an earlier passionate attachment to the American poet, Walt Whitman) he found a perfect (and seemingly willing) candidate. When, in November 1878, Irving secured the lease on the Lyceum Theatre in London, he asked Stoker to become business manager of the theatre. Stoker eagerly accepted the invitation. He threw in his respectable job and, in December 1878, hurriedly married his fiancée, Florence Balcombe (who numbered Oscar Wilde among her former suitors but clearly reckoned Stoker a better bet). The couple left Ireland for London, where their only son, Noel, was born in 1879.

We have a lot more information about this part of Stoker's life. He 'looked after' Irving (or the 'Guvnor' as he was known) for twenty-eight years – a devotion that it is often claimed cost Stoker his relationship with Florence, who resented her husband's being at Irving's beck and call. One American reporter, seeing Stoker going about his job, suggested that his role was 'to occupy some anomalous position between secretary and valet; whose manifest duties are to see that there is mustard in the sandwiches and to take the dogs out for a run....'[25] Somehow, Stoker also found time to make an active literary career for himself, writing over thirty short stories and twelve novels. He moved in influential circles and knew some of the most eminent politicians of his time: W. E. Gladstone, Benjamin Disraeli, Herbert Asquith and Winston Churchill. He also corresponded with such literary figures as Alfred, Lord Tennyson, as well as Oscar Wilde, Arthur Conan Doyle, Mary Braddon, Lucy Clifford and most especially Hall Caine, who spoke of their 'loyal comradeship'.[26] When he worked at the Lyceum he knew the playwrights (including W. S. Gilbert and George Bernard Shaw) and the actors (including Ellen Terry and Genevieve Ward) of his day. When the Lyceum company collapsed in 1902 and other theatrical ventures failed, Stoker turned full-time to writing (almost half Stoker's fictional output belongs to the last seven years of his life). In 1905 Irving died. Stoker, who described himself as the great actor's 'widow', distracted himself by preparing his own tribute, *The Personal*

Reminiscences of Henry Irving (1906), a typically voluminous work of Edwardian hagiography. The *Reminiscences* are one of the most profitable sources of information about Stoker, or at least the way he wanted to be remembered, and he recounts examples of his own remarkable importance, quick thinking, devotion, honesty and tact, at once implying his own superiority to Irving whilst also representing himself as his loyal subject, a stance he retained to the last.

By the early 1900s Stoker's own health had begun to fail. It has been suggested that he suffered from Bright's Disease (a degenerative kidney disease) as early as 1897; in 1906 he suffered a paralyzing stroke, followed by some kind of physical collapse in 1910. We also have some significant small details – such as his appeal to the Royal Literary Fund in 1911, complaining of financial problems. He died on 20 April 1912, aged sixty-four, the official verdict being 'exhaustion'.[27] Yet whilst Stoker lived a very public existence at the heart of late-Victorian theatrical and literary culture, many aspects of his life and personality remain shrouded in mystery. What experiences, it is often asked, shaped his fantastic, often lurid, artistic visions? Did he have a double life like his compatriot and contemporary, Oscar Wilde? Did he love or loathe his employer, Henry Irving? How 'vampiric' was their relationship? I cite these questions not because they are the most useful ones to ask but because they are examples of the lurid speculation Stoker's life often provokes – much of it tied up with *Dracula*. A good deal of new biographical information about him has come to light thanks to works by Barbara Belford, Peter Haining and Peter Tremayne, David Glover and William Hughes.[28] It is fairly clear, however, that there is more to be discovered about his life and career.

STUDYING STOKER

There have been many different approaches to Bram Stoker. The present study is based on two main assumptions. The first is that although it would be wrong to offer an account of Bram Stoker's life and work without talking about his most famous novel, *Dracula*, Stoker's achievements as a writer do not rest solely on this work. *Dracula* was not an aberration; it did not just 'appear' in 1897. As we shall see in the next chapter, Stoker had a long career as a novelist and short-story writer, which began in the early 1870s and lasted until his death in 1912. Although it is impossible in a book of this length to do justice to such a volume of writing, one of the aims of this book is to reveal something of Stoker's diversity as a writer in terms of genre, form and subject matter, thereby suggesting that he is not as easy to pigeonhole as he first seems. Whilst acknowledging the importance that present-day readers ascribe to *Dracula*, this study suggests that there are other dimensions to Stoker's work that are worth acknowledging.

The second main assumption governing this book is that the responses of Stoker's own contemporaries to his novels, and the late-Victorian and Edwardian historical and literary contexts in which he produced his works, are central to any understanding of them. So this book argues for the significance of original appropriations of Stoker, a writer who can seem much gentler and more conservative than the one purloined by twentieth-century film-makers, and especially so when the reader is willing to move beyond the realms of *Dracula* and admit the existence of the other types of work. There is a tension between these different versions of Stoker – between the modern Stoker of the 'here and now' and Stoker the professional writer, whose diverse output is indelibly linked to the popular fictional genres of the late-nineteenth and early-twentieth centuries, to trends in publishing practice and literary fashion, to particular market demands and, above all, to specific historical circumstances and late-Victorian and Edwardian attitudes. It is very difficult to make much sense of Stoker's work without some understanding of the socio-political issues of his time (these are discussed at greater length in the next chapter). There is, it should be said, some debate as to what these issues are, but this book will focus on the issue of identity as it relates to contemporary debates about class, nationhood and gender and the way in which the texts can be said to connect to some of these concerns. It will also suggest that Stoker is a more complex novelist than he initially appears. Although it is very easy to read Stoker as a conservative novelist, one of the attractions of his writing is its polyphony and its potential to resist fixed readings. His work provides examples of the way in which, to quote Tony Bennett, 'popular culture' – and Stoker's novels fall into this category – is 'the terrain on which dominant, subordinate and oppositional cultural values and ideologies meet and intermingle.'[29] Despite Stoker's seeming conventionality and place within the Anglo-centric culture of his time, his writing is interesting for the ways in which it can be read as entering into a fluctuating relationship with the cultural values it appears to espouse. Themes of transgression, rebellion and secrecy regularly appear alongside a fascination with disguise, duplicity and the hidden or split personality.

In a book of this length it is necessary to be selective and, in deciding what issues and texts to concentrate on, I have noted David Glover's recent observation that when studying Stoker, it is very difficult to 'vouchsafe a "definite answer" and we are invariably left with a feeling of incompleteness or omission'.[30] The four chapters that follow are thematically-based and discuss selected issues in relation to Bram Stoker's life and a range of writings produced at different points in his career. By its very nature, a short study of this kind dealing with such varied and multivalent texts (the work of a man who was himself enormously complicated and contradictory) can only offer a small selection of the many different ideas and issues raised by these works. The discussions offered here of particular novels and short stories are intended to whet the reader's appetite. Of the texts chosen, some – like *Dracula* (1897) – have been the focus of a good deal of criticism and my discussion incorporates some of this insightful work; others like *The Primrose Path* (1875) and *Miss Betty* (1898) have received virtually no attention. Broadly speaking, the approach taken is historicist and draws upon the ideas espoused by theorists such as Fredric Jameson and John Cawelti that popular fictional genres – the Gothic novel or the adventure novel, for example – carry a 'socio-symbolic message', that it is possible to discern 'the political unconscious' of a particular text, the ingredients and plot formulas of which change according to particular historical circumstances.[31]

Chapter 1 traces some of the developments in Stoker's critical fortunes and explores some of the ways in which critics have sought to get to grips with Stoker the man. Chapter 2 considers three novels which take London as their main setting; it traces the themes of invasion and identity – male and female – in these works, as well as looking at some of the ways in which Stoker, as a writer within the literary marketplace, also works within the narrative structures and traditions peculiar to different fictional sub-genres of his day. It seeks to demonstrate some of the ways in which Stoker's texts engage with social issues, which had a special relevance in the period – the Empire, degeneration, and women's roles and the family. Read alongside these contexts, these works begin to take on new dimensions, emerging as records of social crisis and their ensuing social conflicts. Chapter 3 continues this theme by considering Stoker's engagement with another popular but highly politicized (and some would argue misogynistic) late-Victorian and Edwardian sub-genre, the adventure romance, together with that genre's interest in defining masculine identity. Chapter 4 looks in more detail at examples of Stoker's novels and short stories in relation to the 'Woman Question' and the extent to which they can be said to dramatize some of the feminist arguments of their day, as well as embodying a male-centred viewpoint. From this analysis will emerge a Stoker who is more varied, powerful and socially aware than many critics have allowed for.

1

Stoker and the Critics

The rise, fall and resurgence of interest in Bram Stoker and his work reflects the changes and fluctuations in literary taste and critical approaches that have taken place over the last 100 years. In his own day Stoker was a well-known man-about-town, doyen of the male world of Victorian clubland, whose stories gave him a reputation as a 'masterful', 'manly' and 'ennobling' writer.[1] The diversity of his work meant that he was compared at various times to Sir Walter Scott, Robert Louis Stevenson and H. G. Wells, whilst some even suggested that it was through his work that the English novel had reached new heights of 'purity'.[2] In 1896, *The Spectator* stressed Stoker's creative originality; this was a novelist who was 'vigorous, clever, pleasant and distinctly out of the common.'[3] In 1897, the conservative *Daily Mail* placed Stoker alongside Marie Corelli, Anthony Hope, Walter Besant, Mary Braddon and Grant Allen in a list of the writers most popular with novel readers.[4] A London newspaper headline of 1907 screamed 'PRURIENT NOVEL IS CONDEMNED, BRAM STOKER OPENS CRUSADE IN LONDON', a response to Stoker's campaign to rid modern fiction of 'impure or dangerous materials'.[5] Yet in the years following his death, attacks on an outlook that came to be regarded as old-fashioned and out-of-date ensured that Stoker was transformed from a figure of respect into one of ridicule.[6]

The publication in 1906 of Stoker's sycophantic (and somewhat self-serving) memoir *The Personal Reminiscences of Henry Irving* helped to intensify the picture of a strict moralist and eager, respectable servant of middle England who, in the supreme act of 'flunkeydom,'[7] propped up the ego of an overrated actor-manager who ruled over the realm of old English theatreland as majestically as Queen Victoria did her own Empire. Stoker's glorification of Irving (and Irving's theatrical triumphs), coupled with his very public outburst in 1908 against the 'startling fact of decadence' in modern fiction, made it very easy to see Stoker as out-of-date, too blinkered and too pompous to speak meaningfully to a modern sensibility.[8] In 1906, in a review of the *Reminiscences*, *Blackwood's Magazine* labelled him a man of 'native simplicity'.[9] For Laurence Irving, the actor's son, Stoker was nothing more than a star-struck 'snob'. Later, in 1919, Irving's son returned to the subject, remembering him as:

> a civil servant...constantly in his [Irving's] company, supping with him off hot lobsters...extravagant...inflated with literary and athletic pretensions [who] worshipped Irving with all the sentimental idolatry of which an Irishman is capable, revelling in the patronage which, as Irving's manager, was at his disposal, and in the opportunities which this position gave him to rub shoulders with the great...vain, impulsive, and inclined to blarneying flattery....[10]

Although one wonders how trustworthy the younger Irving's recollections are, his intentions seem clear enough. He sought to make Stoker look foolish and self-serving, and does so by making fun of his transgression of three fiercely-protected boundaries: taste, nationality and art. Irving thus singles out, for example, Stoker's penchant for exotic seafood, which he presents as evidence of Stoker's greed and his need to live, vampire-like, off the successes of those more talented than himself. By emphasizing the noisy, larger-than-life persona generated by Stoker's 'blarney', Irving presents him as vulgar, lacking in subtlety, and obsessed by celebrities. As an Irishman of lower middle-class origins, Irving's constructed Stoker cannot possibly have mastered the intricacies of good taste and refinement of either manners or art. Even when he does get published, the 'civil servant' Stoker's lack of intellect is all too evident and his works are hardly worth taking seriously (the implication is that no-one did anyhow). From this perspective, Stoker's fictional career is also, of course, an outlet for his overweening ambition when (in Irving's view) serving the Great Actor should have been recognition enough. Laurence Irving is unable to deny the existence of Stoker and his achievements either as an administrator or a writer and therefore attempts to contain him by deriding his manners and depicting him as a hanger-on and social climber.

In contrast, and although renowned for his own snobbery, Hall Caine was (as we saw in the previous chapter) able to discuss Stoker's achievements without depicting him as a self-serving 'hanger-on'.[11] Having said this, Caine's tribute 'Bram Stoker: The Story of a Great Friendship' (1912) establishes a picture of Stoker as a man whose greatest gift was (as the article's title suggests) for 'friendship' with great men like Irving (and by implication Caine himself). Stoker himself was unimportant – measured against the scale of what mattered to Caine and Irving. 'In [this] one thing', Caine announced loftily, 'our poor Bram who had many limitations was truly great.' More significantly – though not surprisingly perhaps given his own self-importance – Caine downplayed the importance of his friend's achievements as a novelist: 'I cannot truly say that [the] deeper side of the man ever expressed itself in his writings. He took no vain view of his efforts as an author...Frankly he wrote his books to sell...he had no higher aims'. The phrases 'no higher aims' and 'written for money' suggests that Stoker's output is made up of ephemeral potboilers, which are of little interest to anyone. 'When I think of his literary output', continued Caine, 'I regret the loss of the one book with which he might have enriched the literature of autobiography. The multitude of interesting persons with whom his position brought him into contact...had left him with vast stores of memories which the public would have welcomed if he had written them down.'[12] Taken together such comments suggest that Bram Stoker's position in early twentieth century culture could simultaneously be an object of admiration (usually on account of his loyalty to Irving) and the butt of jokes (sometimes for the same reason) but as a subject in his own right he was not particularly interesting. The idea that anyone would ever write a book solely devoted to Stoker, and especially about his work as a writer of fiction, seemed eccentric or at least unnecessary.

It is interesting to speculate why Stoker was so little regarded in the years after his death. In one obvious sense, the decline and subsequent revival of interest in Stoker and his work is indicative of the kinds of shifts and changes in taste and understanding that Hans Robert Jauss details in his important study *Towards an Aesthetic of Reception* (1982). Using Jauss's terms, we could argue that the lack of interest in Stoker at the beginning of the twentieth century can be attributed to a change in the 'horizon of expectations' and an 'altered aesthetic norm' that caused 'the audience [to] experience formerly successful works as outmoded and [to] withdraw its appreciation.'[13] Stoker was recognized (perhaps wrongly) for much of his own lifetime as a comforting voice of late-Victorian convention; but when the reaction against things Victorian arrived in the first decades of the twentieth century, he seemed a ready candidate for the critical scaffold. He was a good deal older than Virginia Woolf, Joseph Conrad, Katherine Mansfield, D. H. Lawrence and Rebecca West – the writers who now made up the new (and merciless) cultural elite. His popularity was fading when modernism began to take shape in the years leading up to the First World War, as 'new expressions, new moulds for our thoughts & feelings' (in Mansfield's words) took over.[14] Nor did Stoker's association with genres deemed sub-literary – romance, Gothic, adventure - help matters. Several of his novels stayed in print into the 1920s but as the 'Great Divide' between high art and mass culture widened, Stoker's achievements ('vampires and human snakes', as the *Daily Telegraph* put it) seemed particularly 'dubious' ones.[15] Elsewhere, H. P. Lovecraft's sense of Stoker as an 'infantile' author of horror stories, whose 'crudely written' works were marred by their 'poor technique', lay behind a good many reactions.[16] Nor, despite his being claimed wholeheartedly (as the *Irish Times* did in 1912) as 'an Irishman of the best type',[17] was it easy to make for Stoker much of a place in the Irish literary revival in the early 1900s. He was seen to fall far short of the passionate gestures of contemporaries like W. B. Yeats, J. M. Synge or George Moore (just as he has continued to do until very recently).[18] As a young man, Stoker skipped off to London as soon as he was able and his career as a novelist was, for the most part, made and formed in the late-Victorian London literary marketplace. Yet we might also see Stoker – an Irishman in London – as a displaced subject, occupying a kind of no man's land – neither one thing nor the other, something that (together with his work) made him appear too unconventional to allow him to be neatly slotted in with the other late-Victorians. This difficulty in categorizing Stoker is perhaps why T. S. Eliot felt he was such an interesting character and why he took *Dracula* ('crawled head downward') as one of the sources for *The Wasteland* (1922).[19]

In spite of Eliot's admiration, it was Maurice Richardson who – in his 1959 essay 'The Psychoanalysis of Ghost Stories' – made the most articulate response to Stoker, via *Dracula*. Convinced of its relevance to contemporary society, he began the project of rehabilitating Stoker – or at least his most famous novel. For Richardson, drawing on Sigmund Freud's claims that 'morbid dread always signifies repressed sexual wishes' and searching for literary works that could be used to highlight supposed Victorian anxieties and hypocrisies, Stoker was a peculiarly suitable case for treatment. His vampire novel embodied 'a quite blatant demonstration of the Oedipus complex' with Dracula as 'a father figure of huge potency'. The central issue in *Dracula* was thus the struggle of the father with his sons for control of the women, which resulted in the novel seeming a 'kind of incestuous, necrophilous oral-and-anal-sadistic all-in-wrestling match'.[20] Although it has been fashionable in some quarters to disparage Richardson and later Freudian critics (whose readings of Stoker's novel are based on a narrow, repetitive and 'unliterary' analysis of *Dracula* as a study in sexual repression) such views were extremely influential in the slow process whereby Stoker was deemed a suitably interesting figure for study by English literature students in British and American universities.

Since then the somewhat embarrassed celebration of Stoker as a one-hit wonder, whose strengths were 'jolly good blood and thunder' and the promise of useful material for analyzing Victorian sexual neuroses, has to some extent been broken up.[21] New interpretations have resulted from a range of other twentieth-century critical developments: the development of Marxist criticism as a mode of intellectual inquiry; an interest in colonial and postcolonial approaches to literary texts; and a growing awareness of the intellectual contexts of Stoker's fiction. A new interest in the historical and cultural frameworks of Stoker's work and its relationships with a range of contemporary discourses has formed the basis for studies by, for example, David Glover, Nicholas Daly, Howard Malchow, William Hughes and Joseph Valente – the latter focusing on Stoker's Irish background.[22] The emergence in the 1970s of a generation of feminist critics who sought to highlight the inconsistencies inherent in Stoker's seemingly conventional, and even misogynistic, depictions of women has added to the number of critical positions. Some like Phyllis Roth, whose *Bram Stoker* (1982) was for a long time unique in its willingness to recognize that the rest of Stoker's output beyond *Dracula* might deserve at least some attention, deploy a psychoanalytic model to discover a repressed male psyche. Others like Carol Senf detect hidden meanings beneath a patriarchal surface, or find subversive re-workings of patriarchal literary conventions.[23] Recently, a new interest in so-called 'non-canonical fiction' (notably the Gothic, the fantastic and the late-Victorian adventure romance) together with the realization, as John Sutherland puts it in his *Companion to Victorian Fiction*, that the 'tiny working areas of the "canon" and the paperbacked "classics" are poor reflections of what the Victorian novel actually meant to the Victorians,' has added to the number of critical positions and the numbers of novels being discussed.[24]

Notwithstanding the lengthy spell in which Stoker all but disappeared from the literary canon, his output as a novelist is more impressive and various than we are often given to understand. His first novella, *The Primrose Path* was serialized in the Dublin-based *Shamrock* magazine in 1875, and in 1999 appeared back in print (for the first time in volume form) alongside the second story written for the *Shamrock*, *Buried Treasures* (1875). Stoker's commitments to Irving then meant that there was a long intermission for most of the 1880s but in the 1890s and 1900s he began writing again: *The Snake's Pass* was published in 1890, followed by *The Watter's Mou* (1894), *The Shoulder of Shasta* (1895), *Dracula* (1897), *Miss Betty* (1898), *The Mystery of the Sea* (1902), *The Jewel of Seven Stars* (1903), *The Man* (1905), *Lady Athlyne* (1908), *The Lady of the Shroud* and his swan song, *The Lair of the White Worm* (1911). It is worth remembering that Stoker wrote at a time that saw the creation of a new mass of readers, following the Education Acts introduced between 1870 and 1890. These Acts led to compulsory elementary education for all and an accompanying expansion in the number of outlets for would-be novelists, notably a flood of new cheap magazines and papers which gave a central place to serialized fiction.[25] Thus, *The Snake's Pass* was sold in 1890 to both the *Cardiff Weekly Mail* and the London-based *The People*. Stoker's depiction of Irish

17

rural life, heroism, pure womanhood and material greed appeared alongside adverts for Clarke's 'World Famous Blood Mixture' ['The blood is the life'] and Murphy's 'Walnut Pomade Hair Restorer', as well as in tandem with other articles and stories by popular authors. Elsewhere, Stoker's diverse output included a contribution to a multi-authored sensation novel, *The Fate of Fenella* (1891–2), and over thirty short stories also written expressly for this expanding magazine market. Eventually he had enough to publish three collections of short stories: *Under the Sunset* (1882), *Snowbound: Records of a Theatrical Touring Party* (1908) and *Dracula's Guest* (1914). Whilst in Ireland he also penned numerous essays and theatre reviews, mostly for the Dublin *Evening Mail* and edited an evening newspaper *The Irish Echo*. His work as Inspector of Petty Sessions, a job that he held for ten years, led him to publish *The Duties of Clerks of Petty Sessions in Ireland* (1879). As a devoted business manager to the great actor-manager Sir Henry Irving (from 1878 to 1905) and based in London, Stoker also had time to write several articles on theatrical subjects, and a much praised and admiring essay 'A Glimpse of America' (1888). He also adapted two of his novels – *Dracula* and *Miss Betty* – for the stage, though he never saw them performed. His final work of non-fiction, *Famous Imposters* (1910), is a series of biographical sketches – of Perkin Warbeck, Frederic Mesmer, Arthur Orton – who craft different 'selves' as a means of 'self-protection', culminating in the claim that Elizabeth I was actually a man in disguise (*FI* 111). The quality of these works varies enormously but the diversity of these achievements is another reminder that Stoker is a figure who cannot be conveniently classified with a single label.

As with the list of Stoker's works, the different interpretative frameworks through which critics now approach him is a reminder of the dimensions of Stoker's achievements and the complex and often open-ended questions his work provokes. That there has always been (and still remains) a difficulty in 'staking' down Stoker owes much to the tension that exists between his roles as orthodox and conservative supporter of the status quo and a writer of garish portrayals of evil and sexual obsession. As critics are now beginning to realize, this also has a great deal to do with the complexity of the novels. As William Hughes rightly points out, Stoker's work is characterized by its 'ability to reflex, to twist its own meaning to another purpose.'[26] The slipperiness that Hughes identifies has been formulated in many ways by recent critics but it includes the tensions between Stoker's seemingly hearty public persona and the emphasis in his novels on the hidden self: the schism within a writer 'nervously glancing back at the past as he...[strode] out into the future' as David Glover puts it, a man caught up in 'the competing attractions of different national identities', as well as the emotional turmoil stemming from his fundamental insecurities.[27]

Glover's comments are a telling reminder that one of the most common consequences of confusion in the interpretation of Stoker's work has been the persistent tendency to read the novels as having autobiographical elements. The parallels between Stoker's own life and his novels – particularly but not exclusively, *Dracula* – have helped to make them compelling works, both for the inquisitive reader and for critics and biographers concerned with Stoker's literary creativity. The notorious ending that Daniel Farson supplied for his 1975 biography *The Man Who Wrote Dracula*, helped to inaugurate this trend. Stoker's fate, Farson concluded, had been to die slowly and painfully from syphilis, contracted in the 1880s when his wife's alleged frigidity forced him to engage the services of prostitutes. Farson suggested that 'his [Stoker's] obsession with horror and the repetition of sexual symbols indicate that Stoker was disturbed.'[28] Leonard Woolf sees in Stoker's work 'the raw harsh presence of a man who is writing over, around and under what he knows about loneliness and – predominantly – sexual terror'. Nowadays such claims to have 'discovered' the 'real' Bram Stoker are met with even more frequently, in scholarly journals and in the popular media. In addition to a pre-Oedipal complex, Stoker has variously been given an 'anxiety neurosis' in regard to menstruating women which makes itself felt in *Dracula* and membership of various secret occult societies practising ritual magic, tied together with what in 2003 cod-psychologists are fond of terming as 'low self esteem'. Elsewhere – in a recent *New York Times* article – Margot Peters, in telling us what Stoker was really 'like', presents him as self-effacing, a perfect middle-managerial type: one who was always content to take the back seat to Henry Irving, but a man who was also bitter and whose 'revenge for life-long self effacement

19

was *Dracula*.[29] Malcolm Sutcliffe in the revealingly-titled *Dracula Revealed: Style, Theme, Archetype and Echoes of Bram Stoker* (1999) writes that Stoker is constantly 'in and amongst his characters'.[30] In a curious way, these stances are a critical throwback to those adopted by Stoker's contemporary reviewers who offloaded their approval of Stoker the gentleman and his status as a 'manly' pillar of the community onto the upright heroes and heroines of his fiction. In a review of *The Mystery of the Sea* (1902) *Punch* observed that 'through it all beams the breezy personality of Bram Stoker.'[31] Later, *The Academy* praised the *Personal Reminiscences* as being typically 'strong' and 'manly' and suggested that 'It is impossible to read unmoved'.[32] In 1897, his reading of *Dracula* prompted C. F. Moberley Bell, the editor of *The Times*, to tell Stoker that 'To read a man's book is the next best thing to talking to him'.[33] Although Bell hesitated in accepting the novel as pseudo-autobiography, many twentieth-century critics have not been so reluctant. Indeed, as a critical habit, it has proved remarkably persistent. It is added grist to the biographer's mill that, in his own lifetime, Stoker explained his own character as deliberately elusive and 'naturally secretive to the world', speaking out against 'the evil force of irresponsible chatter' (*PR* I ix). In reading Stoker's fiction, it is often assumed (without much evidence) that the narrator is the author or that a particular character is a 'mouthpiece' for Stoker or that s/he is a psychological slip on Stoker's part. The very obvious limitations of these kinds of reading and of the difficulties in locating the 'real' Bram Stoker become evident as the extent and diversity of his achievements are recognized more fully.

Talia Schaffer's important 1994 essay, 'A Wilde Desire Took Me: The Homoerotic History of *Dracula*'[34] walks this critical tightrope. The essay is traditional in its concern for Stoker's life but modern in the context of recent developments in gender studies. Schaffer's work, along with that of Ed Cohen, can be said to exemplify the way in which queer theory has been used to explore the homosexual dimension of works produced when homosexuality could not be candidly acknowledged. Schaffer is interested in the question of language, but from the perspective of what is absent, displaced or coded. Following Cohen, she poses the question: how is it possible for an 'ec-centric' [i.e. homosexual] Victorian man to express his 'true' self or 'otherness' in a society where such difference cannot speak its name?[35] *Dracula, The Personal Reminiscences of Henry Irving* and Stoker's gushing letters to male friends Walt Whitman and Hall Caine are chosen by Schaffer as works which can be picked apart to permit the tracing 'not [of] Stoker's sexual history but the textual history of Stoker's repressed sexuality'. According to Schaffer, 'Stoker's particular textual codes express homoerotic passion through repriation, invocations of openness and accounts of his hidden hysteria', especially where Irving and Whitman were concerned. In her reading of *Dracula*, Schaffer analyses what she takes to be Stoker's ambiguous silence during and after the public humiliation, trial and imprisonment of Oscar Wilde for sodomy in 1895: 'He writes as a man victimized by Wilde's trial and yet as a man who sympathizes with Wilde's victimization.' This sympathy makes itself felt in various forms in the novel but most obviously in the scenes surrounding the presentation of the vampire who is 'a kind of basin in which images of Wilde-as-monster float...the ghoulish inflated version of Wilde produced by Wilde's prosecutors; the corrupting, evil, secretive, manipulative corruptor of little boys'. Although Schaffer does not claim that Dracula is merely a crude pen portrait of Wilde, she does suggest that the Count is a 'monstrous, dirty, threatening...elegy for the enforced intern-ment of [Stoker's own] desires'. Within the confines of this kind of reading, such voyeuristic 'lapses' on Stoker's part can be read as the 'homotextuality', to use Byrne Fone's description, characteristic of so-called gay texts of the period.[36] They raise the issue of a 'gay observer's' access to power and knowledge, and how notions of homosexuality are articulated within pre-existing (male) discourse.[37] Schaffer's move from a subtle analysis of the texts to the larger theoretical debate, via Eve Sedgwick, has made this a much-quoted essay in Stoker criticism, with its pressing questioning of how Stoker was able (or not) to disentangle himself from the concepts that bound him. Schaffer's essay is also, of course, useful in another way, namely that it suggests the adaptability of Stoker's writing to different kinds of readings. As we shall see, Stoker's writings can just as easily be read 'straight', that is they can produce a different (heterosexual) interpretation; equally it is possible that there may be hints in the text which point to ways in which another interpretative community – a male homosexual audience – could be specifically targeted.[38]

Whilst we can no longer resort to a simple amalgamation of the life and the work to dismiss Stoker's work as involuntary self-revelation, many critics continue to find this kind of biographical approach difficult to avoid. Joseph Bierman's 'A Critical Stage in the Writing of Dracula', one of the essays appearing in William Hughes and Andrew Smith's important collection, *Bram Stoker: History, Psychoanalysis and the Gothic* (1998), is a case in point. This essay applies psychoanalytic principles to Stoker's works, presenting us with a detailed case study of the novelist. Thus one of the ways in which Bierman reads *Dracula* and the short tales contained in *Under the Sunset*, published in 1882, is as examples of Stoker's 'organizing childhood fantasy of the...*claustrum*, which represents the interior of the mother's body as an orally regressive safe haven....' The texts also become expressions of 'conflict and anxiety about his heterosexual and homosexual...wishes' and in Bierman's reading it is the children's stories in *Under the Sunset*, written for Stoker's son, Noel, but also packaged for the 1882 Christmas market, which take centre stage.[39] The setting for these allegorical tales is a mythic land, bordered by a dark wilderness, ruled over by the King of Death. In 'The Shadow Builder', Stoker describes a battle between the Shadow Builder (who is figured as Death) and the Mother (who represents Life). The Mother, the guarantor of identity, tries to keep her son from the future, Death, and from the mysterious space in between Life and Death called 'THE THRESHOLD', where 'all things lose their being and become part of the great Is-Not... Whatever passes into it, disappears; and whatsoever emerges from it is complete as it comes and passes into the great world as a thing to run its course.'[40] Drawing on the patterns suggested by structuralism and the patterns of Jungian psychoanalysis, Bierman suggests that it is the male baby who functions as a carrier of the author's unconscious personality. Bierman also displays the need to find an angry or dissatisfied Bram Stoker lurking in the text. He argues that *Under the Sunset*, even more than *Dracula*, is a work haunted by Stoker's personal ghosts. Both, according to Bierman, are texts which emphasize obsessively the safety to be found in enclosed spaces (coffins, tombs, locked rooms). The short story 'How 7 Went Mad' is 'a derivative version of Stoker's memories of and fantasies about his childhood illness' in which he was bled, the bloodletting being 'experienced by him first as being eaten up, and then as a castration anxiety.' The unnamed and unmanned child in this story, whose life, like that of the young bed-ridden Stoker, is characterized by isolation, was, Bierman suggests, particularly relevant to Stoker at the time of the story's composition. Working for Irving, he was still 'unable to stand on his own two feet or to stand erect in the physical or the phallic sense'. Alongside Schaffer's essay, Bierman's reading offers perhaps the most provocative analysis of the relationship between text and author's life and certainly one very different from those that appeared in the aftermath of his death.

Whilst many critics continue to find a good deal of mileage in psychoanalytic readings of the novels – readings that tend to be essentialist and non-historical – others adopt a socio-political approach. There is the same curiosity as to the instability of meanings, signs and metaphors in the novels but it manifests itself in an emphasis on Stoker's centrality within the history of *fin de siècle* fears and ideas. This is the case with Jeffrey Richards in his essay 'Gender and Class in Bram Stoker's Other Novels' (1996). Like Bierman, Richards is interested in the obstructions to Stoker's growth and development – notably Irving – but whereas Bierman is interested in Stoker's novels as evidence of personal neuroses, Richards focuses on the ways in which Stoker's novels can be seen to be 'plugged into the main currents of anxiety' of his day.[41] These anxieties were considerable. Over-crowding, poverty, poor standards of national health, widespread unemployment, falling birth rates, syphilis, mass alcoholism and the increasing momentum of the woman's movement fostered a sense that *fin de siècle* Britain was in the throes of 'social decrepitude'.[42] Economic, commercial and political competition on the world stage from the USA and Germany, together with the difficulties in maintaining Britain's imperial rule, further added to the sense that the country was being exhausted by colonial expansion. Confirmation of this seemed to come with the long campaigns of the Boer War (1899–1900), one of the effects of which was to highlight glaring deficiencies in Britain's military capability. A sense of Englishness gone bad helped to create an interest in eugenics and prompted calls for immigration to be carefully monitored. The novelist H. Rider Haggard wrote scathingly in 1905 of 'puny pigmies growing from towns or town-bred parents.'[43] Visiting England in 1907, the Australian Minister for External Affairs, Billy Hughes, announced that Britain's moral and spiritual life were rotten at the core and 'the rottenness is spreading like a cancer through every fibre of the social organism.'[44] One of the most infamous texts of the period, Max Nordau's *Degeneration* (1895), described (in terms which seem to foreshadow Count Dracula's arrival in England) how: '...the clouds are aflame... Over the earth the shadows creep with deepening gloom, wrapping all objects in a mysterious dimness, in which all certainty is destroyed and any guess seems plausible. Forms lose their outlines, and are dissolved in floating mist. The day is over, the night draws on.'[45] The result was 'moral seasickness' and the 'unchaining of the beast in man'. Read alongside these contexts, the undead, the doppelgänger, the bestial people, the sexually aggressive, rebellious women of Stoker's novels begin to take on new dimensions, emerging, as components of a very topical 'literature of terror',[46] one that taps into a shared sense of abject social crisis and an ensuing social conflict, at the same time as suggesting ways of managing them.[47] It is worth noting that when they were first published, some of Stoker's early works – *The Snake's Pass*, *Miss Betty*, *The Mystery of the Sea*, even *Dracula* – were praised by some readers for their high moral tone and their uplifting evocation of an unstable, troubled society, one which is restored to health when a heroic group of men and women band together to defeat some monstrous challenge to the stability of Western (English) civilization. In 1897, Mrs Boyd Carpenter, wife of the Bishop of Ripon, wrote to Stoker praising *Dracula* as 'an allegory of sin' directed against 'those whose belle-lettres repel'.[48] As we shall see in chapter 4, one of the reasons behind the historical novel *Miss Betty*'s popularity was that it could be read as a pastoral idyll, which displaced the tensions of 1897 by projecting an idealized world of the early 1700s. Thus, a writer for the *North British Review* exhibited nostalgia for the time Stoker depicted so evocatively, a 'simple and charming romance of the reigns of Queen Anne and George I' and a story of 'a woman's devotion'.[49] With a society in flux, one can hardly be surprised at such nostalgia for a more static and ordered way of life.

The notion that Stoker's novels should be read as metaphorical condensations of specific anxieties faced by the English upper and middle classes in the 1890s and 1900s forms part of a wider trend within contemporary Victorian studies in situating literature within history – a history understood not in the simplistic manner of 'background' but instead as 'cultural text, which is the matrix or master code that the literary text both depends upon and modifies.'[50] Although this kind of work was initially associated most frequently with the study of the English Renaissance, any period can be examined in this way and the transitional state of late nineteenth-century society which Stoker represents, together with his own recently proven interest in political and social debate, has been seen to offer a good deal of potential for this kind of approach.[51] In the 1990s work by Daniel Pick, Rhys Garnett, Stephen Arata, Andrew Smith, David Glover and William Hughes was influential in helping to set a precedent for viewing Stoker's fiction from the perspective of its wider social, economic and political contexts, linking, for example, the events and characters of the novels to the question of representation in all kinds of writings – newspaper reports, political speeches, journalism, medical texts, conduct books, novels – produced by his contemporaries. What the present study is interested in is the extent to which Stoker's novels, like other texts written in the same period, can be said to have been shaped by the social structures and ideological sources of the 1890s and 1900s. This period saw the rise of a consumerist society, urbanization, the conflict between the old and the new, between men and women, and between the declining older land-owning classes and a new powerful social group – the professional bourgeoisie. As we shall see, Stoker quite clearly draws attention to his characters' position within a society that is on the cusp of modernity and the way that this society impinged upon the development of the individual – male and female.

One immediate discursive context for Stoker's fiction, as it is discussed in the present study, is the urgency with which late nineteenth and early twentieth-century writers continued to debate the figure of the middle-class woman. In 'Modern

Women' (1895), the German feminist Laura Marholm wrote of a 'new phase in woman's nature'.[52] A decade later, in Maud Churton Braby, author of the popular advice manual *Modern Marriage and How to Bear It* (1908) likewise observed 'a spirit of strange unrest' among women.[53] One manifestation of this was an emphasis on the disconcerting figure of the 'New Woman' and debates about women's rights, duties, feelings, sexuality, independence. Stoker's seemingly unresolved stance on these issues makes him an interesting subject for analysis. This is doubly so when we consider some of the important critical frameworks for thinking about the representation of women in texts written by Victorian men that have been provided by feminist critics. Kate Millett famously argued in *Sexual Politics* (1970), that the misrepresentation and misogyny inherent in images of women in male-authored literary works originates in men's need to retain sexual and political control over women. 'Good' women, she noted, are often assigned positive nurturing qualities that suggest their suitability for lives of motherhood and domesticity – lives that tend to be glorified and thus 'serve as models for a broader process of pacification'.[54] This is an idea taken up by Toril Moi in *Sexual Textual Politics* (1985), where she notes that: 'patriarchal oppression consists of imposing certain social standards of femininity on all biological women, in order precisely to make us believe that the chosen standards for "femininity" are natural, that a woman who refuses to conform can be labeled both unfeminine and *unnatural*.'[55] According to this line of thought, binary oppositions and the representations they involve have always been used by male novelists to help justify male patriarchal authority and the often violent methods used to sustain it.

Moi also notes that women in fiction act as 'spaces' onto which men project their own fears and anxieties about female sexuality. 'But behind the angel lurks the monster: the obverse of the male idealization of women is the male fear of femininity. The monster woman is the woman who refuses to be selfless, acts on her own initiative...a woman who rejects the submissive role patriarchy has reserved for her'.[56] What this also means, of course, is that 'beneath the ample heaps of contempt...foisted on women by men' feminist critics have been able to uncover 'signs of feared female potentials and struggles', what Michael Ryan, in a useful summary, describes as the horrible 'counter-possibility – that women might be more powerful than men.'[57] The genres for which Stoker is most famous – horror, the supernatural, the Gothic – are often taken as fertile sites for this kind of misogynistic representation. However, one of the concerns of this book will be to consider some of the ways in which images of women in Stoker's texts, and the plots of female destiny foisted on female characters, may offer glimpses of the way that late-Victorian and Edwardian male power was maintained through representation and stereotype, at the same time that they also suggest the insecurities underlying this operation. At the same time, in looking at Stoker's representation of women, we should not overlook the fact that there may also, as Ruth Robbins has recently suggested in *Literary Feminisms*, be ways in which 'a masculine version of femininity is not merely a conformist or conservative version; such a version may open up and become subversive of the patriarchy which has created it.'[58] In taking up these issues of gender and gender representation, one of the questions that I want to consider is whether Stoker merely dramatizes and perpetuates some of the stereotypes of women available in the late nineteenth and early twentieth centuries or whether in fact he undermines them? Are his fictions examples of what Laura Claridge and Elisabeth Langland have termed the 'male feminist voice?'[59]

In 2003 the diverse critical reactions to Stoker and his work show no sign of abating. The critical frameworks discussed in this chapter reveal that a number of very different Bram Stokers exist and co-exist. These different constructions of Stoker are the result of cultural positions being constantly formed and held, challenged and subverted, but also of Stoker's own complexity as a writer and an accompanying recognition that we cannot see him simply as the author of only one novel, *Dracula*. This same complexity means, of course, that the directions in which future criticism on Stoker might go are numerous. For example, if critics in 2003 are just as concerned with the psychoanalytic potential of the novels as they were thirty years ago, they are now more alert to their involvement in the creation of social discourse and to the contemporary anxieties Stoker's writings may manipulate or conceal. The next chapter will consider some of these in greater detail, especially as they relate to issues of gender and the role of women. It will also develop the idea that we need to be conscious of the literary and economic milieu in which Stoker's novels were produced – that is, the literary field of late-Victorian and Edwardian London – as well as of the different literary sub-genres within which he worked. The recognition that his writing was a form of labour, that publishing is a business and that the shape of Stoker's novels was marked by these material facts – and by his envy of the mass readership enjoyed by his friends Hall Caine, Arthur Conan Doyle and Mary Braddon, should not be overlooked. As we become more alert to the ideological and 'cultural functions' of popular literary culture, re-discover popular novelists of the late nineteenth and early twentieth centuries, and become less tied to notions of canonicity, we should, as I hope to show, find Stoker's work interesting for its variety, its contradictions, and its attempt to participate in literary trends of the period and its clear appeal to Victorian and Edwardian readers.

2

London in View

London is the setting for several of Bram Stoker's novels and in this chapter we will examine three of the most striking of these works. The texts – *The Primrose Path,* published in 1875, *Dracula,* published in 1897, and *The Jewel of Seven Stars,* published in 1903 – can be taken as examples of Stoker's work at three different periods of his career. They also demonstrate something of his ability to write within different genres. *The Primrose Path* is a temperance (anti-alcohol) novel and 'emigration parable'[1]; *Dracula* is a vampire novel, and also uses some of the tropes of the imperial Gothic and the fantastic; and *The Jewel of Seven Stars* is an Orientalist, Gothic novel, which exploits the mystique and exoticism of Ancient Egypt. The setting for these novels – London – was where Stoker himself lived, from 1878 until his death in 1912. As he puts it in *Dracula*: 'mighty London', 'I had the idea of going to London...I long[ed] to go through the crowded streets...to be in the midst of the whirl and rush of humanity, to share its life, its change, its death, and all that makes it what it is.' (*D* 50–1) It would be in London, Stoker recalled, that 'as a writer I should have a larger scope and better chance of success than at home.' (*PR* 44).

One of the striking things about all these texts is that they give us a rather double-edged view of the capital. London is a stronghold of civilization but also a place that is extremely vulnerable to attack and can be a place[d] danger. Both *Dracula* and *The Jewel of Seven Stars* convey this in fairly lurid and 'fantastic' ways, starting off in the strange and alien worlds of Transylvania and Ancient Egypt but then depicting how their monsters have risen up to find their way to London, the supposed impregnable centre of the modern world. Showing the terrifying eruption of the supernatural and other spectres of

29

monstrosity – demonic females, doubles, taboo desires, themes of infectious disease, unlawful (sexual) desires, subterranean spaces – all packaged together in a fragmented narrative and sometimes confusing narrative structure, Stoker uses many of the conventions of what we have come to recognize as Gothic writing. However, Stoker's texts differ from late eighteenth-century manifestations of the Gothic novel in which the sinister is kept at a safe distance by being located in an exotic location far away. Stoker's fantasy fictions, which critics have sometimes labelled 'Urban Gothic', describe the intrusion of the monstrous taking place much closer to home, revealing what Henry James famously termed 'those most mysterious of mysteries, the mysteries which are at our own doors...infinitely the more terrible'.[2] When the malevolent mummy, Queen Tera, appears in an innocent-looking Notting Hill house in *The Jewel of Seven Stars*, the initial reaction of the characters is one of disbelief and a kind of blind terror at discovering that the monstrous is real and preparing to take possession of their civilized modern city. It is not Ancient Egypt but London, England, which is the site of monstrosity. More ominously, as Stoker shows in *Dracula*, when Jonathan Harker thinks the Count is standing behind him but looks in the mirror and sees only his own reflection, the monsters are only 'catalysts which allow the latent monstrosity to emerge. The monster is in the civilized English character, lurking in the "self"; the monster is Victorian England.'[3]

Stoker's own dreams of metropolitan life seem to have been well-satisfied. A character in *The Primrose Path* points out: 'if you want to make money, London's the place' (*PP* 29) and Stoker's own income and lavish lifestyle suggests that he did just this in the 1880s and 1890s, establishing a comfortable base for himself and Florence. London, he felt, was his 'natural and immediate habitat.' For Stoker, as for another literary *arriviste* Henry James, all the doors in London were opened to the 'freedom and ease, knowledge and power, money, opportunity and satiety' of which the 'swarming facts' of London spoke.[4] By the time he came to write *Dracula*, Stoker could market himself with some complacency as a 'Londoner of twenty years standing' who 'knew everybody worth knowing' in the glittering worlds of literature, art, theatre and politics.[5] As I have mentioned, he was a man whose life was bound up with the Lyceum Theatre, a cultural institution that Stoker recalled in the *Personal Reminiscences* as embodying 'the spirit mastering the heartbeat of that great Empire on which the sun never sets' (*PR* I 342).[6] However, there were, as Stoker noted, 'counterfoils' to all this (*PP* 49). In the short story 'Crooken Sands' (1894) he writes of the 'roar of London – the darkness...and weariness of London life' (*DG* 175). Few people could shut their eyes to the fact that under the trappings of civilization there lurked a crude barbarism. Events such as the 'Jack the Ripper' murders of 1888, the Cleveland Street Scandal in 1889 (which revealed a homosexual brothel) and W. H. Stead's exposé of child prostitution in 'The Maiden Tribute of Modern Babylon' (1885) had uncovered a darker side to the 'needs and habits of a great city' as Stoker describes them in *The Jewel of Seven Stars* (*JSS* 3). We see similar worries in Stoker's lecture *A Glimpse of America* (1886), in which he describes how the English are reverting to a primitive state – 'aboriginals' rather than colonists. 'We Londoners...have points of contact with as high a civilization as the earth affords; and also, I fear, with here and there, as complete a system of savagery as distinguished those aborigines who won a place in history by resting on the outside of Captain Cook.' (*GA* 5)

Stoker's novels can thus be read as texts that convey some of the strains generated by the contradictions at work at the 'heart of empire': a widespread sense that technological progress was ushering in a modernity which conflicted with the cultural values long-held dearly by the previous generation: stability, integrity, patriotism, moral uprightness. Whilst his own background was, he claimed, that of 'a conservative in a conservative country [i.e. Ireland]',[7] he could appreciate the power and energy of the new. Few nineteenth-century texts look towards the twentieth century and the dynamics of modernity as much as *Dracula*. Chasing the Count across Europe, for example, Dr Seward regrets having to use such primitive forms of communication as the pen: 'How I miss my phonograph'; this sense of restlessness, new technology and rapid change is echoed by Jonathan Harker in his diary where he realizes that this is 'the nineteenth century up-to-date with a vengeance'. But he also realizes rather more ominously that 'the old centuries had, and have, powers of their own which mere "modernity" cannot kill' (*D* 67).

As we noted in the previous chapter, a popular – some might say reductive – way of reading Stoker's texts is to suggest that they tap into a wide-ranging 1890s sense of cultural malaise[8] and that, like Gothic novels more generally, they do so in a way which is designed to heighten the fears of their audience. Stoker is particularly interested in the relationship between the past and the present and with the implications of the past for 'civilized' Europeans, including the possibility that modern man (or woman) could devolve as well as progress, and his work is shot through with degenerationalist anthropology, common at the *fin de siècle*. Moreover, fears about the bestial heritage of humanity, atavism, and sexuality are all underlined by a nightmare vision of the capital city (which represents civilization), threatened by the inexorable encroachment of the primitive forces of the uncivilized world and the repressed unconscious looming up out of the darkness.[9] As David Glover points out: 'London was increasingly becoming the symbolic place in the late-Victorian and Edwardian imaginaries where boundaries threatened to dissolve.'[10] Stoker draws attention to his characters' positions within a changing social structure and he follows not only those who succeed but those who fail and are consumed by the city. In *The Primrose Path*, Jerry O'Sullivan's social ruin is stated within a Darwinian frame of reference which, with its focus on the dark side of industrial capitalist culture embodied in a particular kind of urban savagery, is then extended in *Dracula*, a text with more than its fair share of 'zoophagous','life-eating' men, and whose heroes 'enter into the feeling of the hunter.'[11] Stoker uses London landmarks – the Zoological Gardens, Hyde Park and Rotten Row, Dracula's house in Piccadilly, the Albermarle Hotel, the Port of London - to create a sense of 'place' but they are also a way of suggesting the kinds of civilized values under attack, as well as forming a sinister terrain of the mind.

THE PRIMROSE PATH

The Primrose Path was the first novel that Stoker wrote (at about the age of 27) and which was accepted for publication. Drafted in the early 1870s, it was revised in 1874 and probably again, before its serialization in the Dublin-based *Shamrock* (February–March 1875). The *Shamrock* was a penny weekly magazine that prided itself on its 'Cheap Literature'.

To date, however, the novel has received very little attention. There are, nevertheless, good reasons for reading *The Primrose Path*, not least for the way in which it acts as a kind of *ur*-source for some of the main concerns of Stoker's other fictions, notably the challenges to identity and selfhood posed by monstrous forces, threats to 'civilized' [middle-class] patterns of behaviour, violence against women, and the clash of cultures. However, *The Primrose Path* can also be fitted into the generic category of the temperance novel – an earnest sub-genre of realist fiction which flooded onto the market in the mid-nineteenth century in both England and Ireland, its popularity the result of middle-class fears that industrialization was not only producing overcrowding, poverty and despair but was turning people to seek solace in alcohol. Anne Brontë's *The Tenant of Wildfell Hall*, a tale of a middle-class woman trapped in marriage to an abusive drunkard had been published in 1848, George Eliot's unusually sympathetic portrayal of a drunken woman, 'Janet's Repentance', in 1857 and Ellen Wood's prizewinning *Danesbury House* in 1860. Temperance imagery also made its way into other major novels of the period including Elizabeth Gaskell's *Mary Barton* (1848) and Charles Dickens' *Oliver Twist* (1837), where the very name of The Three Cripples tavern signals the moral atrophy of Bill Sykes and everyone else who frequents it.[12]

In *The Primrose Path*, Jerry O'Sullivan, an Irish carpenter, moves to London with his wife, Katey, lured over by an old friend John Seebright and the promise of better wages. He falls into the sinister clutches of Mons, an actor in the back-street theatre where Jerry is employed, Gemmell, a publican and then alcohol itself. At first a 'gift' from Mons, then a servant (used to restore Jerry to consciousness after a fight), alcohol soon becomes the most tyrannical of masters, and the hero its 'unconscious tool' (*PP* 98). The plot's moral aesthetic encourages us to believe that once he has begun to drink, Jerry's economic and social collapse into 'hopeless misery' (*PP* 62) is an inevitable one – as inevitable as the deaths which follow. In a gruesome climax, Jerry kills Katey in a drunken rage before slitting his own throat.

In their depiction of the ravages of alcohol, temperance novelists tended to do three things: firstly, to make a spectacle of the diseased physiology associated with drinking and to show how every mishap in the narrative pertained to the ill results of intemperance; secondly, to show how opposed were the twin pillars of the community, the public house and the home; and thirdly to stress the subversive social forces unleashed by alcohol.[13] These elements were packaged together in a sensationalist discourse inherited from the lurid magazine stories, the so-called 'penny-dreadfuls' and from melodrama. Stoker's novel actually heightens horror with the populist Stoker utilizing all the shock tactics of temperance fiction to make his point. Jerry O'Sullivan degenerates into a father who batters his family physically and economically. Alcohol leads inexorably to unemployment, physical degradation, poverty and death. 'See', readers are urged, 'the pale drunken wasted-looking men, with sunken eyes, and slouching gait. Men that were once strong and hard-working and upright....Look at them now! Afraid to meet your eyes, trembling at every sound; mad with passion one moment and with despair the next.' (*PP* 26–7) This kind of exhortation is a reminder that nineteenth-century temperance stories reached gloomy conclusions about the effects of drink, presenting drinking as a sign of moral weakness and the drinker as the subject of a moral defect. As anti-drink messages, temperance novels were meant, sermon-like, to show 'wretched' drunkards their sinful ways and to reinforce the idea that only a life of sobriety would bring financial and social security, that 'if there were no spirits there would be less sin, and shame and sorrow than there is.' (*PP* 27) The title of Stoker's novel, *The Primrose Path* and its chapter headings – 'Down the Hill', 'The Trail of the Serpent', The End of the Journey' – are indicative of the direction of its moral thrust and its links to such traditional allegorical and didactic texts as John Bunyan's *Pilgrim's Progress* (1678) and The *Life and Death of Mr Badman* (1680). In addition, these chapter headings give prior warning of the novel's suggestion that, consciously or otherwise, men and women shape their own destinies.

At the same time, *The Primrose Path*, which begins with Jerry Sullivan's impulsive decision to seek his fortune in London, is a story, not just of drink, but of egotism, over-reaching ambition and self deception: 'eyes – the eyes of his inner self...so full of his project that they were incapable of seeing anything but what bore on its advancement. He shut his eyes to danger and defects and difficulties and like many another man leaped blindly into the dark' (PP 38). This impulsiveness and lack of judgement driven by 'the power of evil' (PP 35) is at the root of the troubles that, according to the internal logic of the temperance genre, destroy the hero, the hero's career, and his wife, Katey and their children. There are two opposing sides to Jerry's personality, which the alcohol causes to rise to the surface. When Jerry returns home drunk, his terrified wife recognizes the footsteps on the stairs as 'her husband's but yet not his' (PP 62). There are suggestions that this aspect of his character represents a kind of innocence and unworldliness, but at other times Jerry's behaviour is more obviously foolish and even self-destructive as, for example, when – against his better judgement – he entrusts himself to Seebright and the others. The plot encourages us to believe that once he has begun to drink, Jerry's economic and social collapse into 'hopeless misery' (PP 62) is an inevitable one – as inevitable as death.

Elsewhere, *The Primrose Path* contains a murder, a suicide, wife-beating, gambling, episodes of delirium tremens – all resulting from the 'hell cauldron' of alcohol. Stoker's readers would have recognized the symbolic interweaving of alcohol and death images as when he describes the barman with his skull-like head. In his description of him, face, half eaten away with 'canker', Stoker may also have been asking readers to recognise the dreaded final stages of syphilis. They would have been familiar with the coupling of drinking and dishonesty in the portrayal of John Seebright and the Dante-esque spiral downwards of the narrative, the images of drinks being poured into dirty tumblers (a sign of the illusory nature of alcohol's pleasures), and they would have seen the appropriateness of Stoker's suggestion that drunkenness both transforms and confirms the working classes as a different 'savage' species from the rest of the human race. Jerry is a social exile with 'clothing tossed and hair unkempt – with a feverous look and bloodshot eyes, drinking his rum..., and taking it from the hand of one who, with solid finery and unwashed face, might have stood for picture of 'Debauch' (PP 89; 88). Jerry is literally monstrous, his appearance an example of what Judith Halber-stam, in her discussion of connections between the Gothic monster's body and the psyche, calls 'a disciplinary sign, a warning of what may happen if the body is imprisoned by its desires or if the subject is unable to discipline him – or herself fully'.[14] Although critics have noticed and analyzed the ways in which Stoker fixates on what happens when characters exceed expected bounds of behaviour (as we shall see, Lucy Westenra in *Dracula* is a notable example of this), the tendency has been to overlook the anxiety they produce in Stoker's earliest works. Temperance novels repeatedly stressed the mental struggle for control experienced by the drunkard and it is possible to see Stoker using Jerry's physical regression as a metaphor for the concerns about discipline and regulation, which were important aspects of masculine identity.

These fears about the loss of independence and selfhood, figured as 'enslavement', are central to an understanding of *The Primrose Path*. Yet whilst they suggest the text's generic links to the temperance novel, they also point more generally in other directions.[15] Although novels that claimed to lay bare what Stoker describes as 'the curse of Ireland' (i.e drink) (*PP* 31) were commonplace, novels that did this whilst simultaneously interrogating the question of authentic national identities in London ('a city where the devil lives') were more unusual. As someone with metropolitan aspirations of his own, Stoker was in a good position to write empathetically of the experiences of Irish immigrants. *The Primrose Path* contains a very evocative description of what it was like for newcomers arriving in London by boat; the sense of 'awe' inspired by 'the strength of the defences...[which] made the idea of any hostile force...a complete impossibility' (*PP* 48). Stoker's own sudden decision to throw in his lot with Irving may have meant that he could also empathize with his hero Jerry O'Sullivan's induction at the hands of an insidious Mephistophelean figure into a mode of life which results in his losing some of his own identity to the demands of another.

As we saw in chapter 1, such psycho-biographical readings are popular in Stoker studies. Yet *The Primrose Path* can also be read as Stoker's response to a highly specific modern indus-trialized culture, the culture of capitalism. As well as warning of the dangers of alcohol, Stoker sets his readers another question: how can one have a contented and secure family life when its spiritual values are so consistently under siege and are so inadequate to the economic forces of industrial capitalism, as they operate in the city? One of the effects of nineteenth-century capitalism was, as Karl Marx and Friedrich Engels argued, the creation of an economic system which brought people together to live and work in close proximity but pitted them against one another.[16] The worker became simply a cog or 'tool' for hire in a huge machine, subservient to a vast, impersonal, dehumanizing, competitive system. In his 1869 study of racial decline, *Hereditary Genius*, the anthropologist Francis Galton likewise commented on 'the draggled, drudged, mean look of the mass of individuals...that one meets in the streets of London.' 'The conditions of their life' he wrote, did not allow for any 'semblance of common humanity.'[17] Read in this context, Stoker's novel, which likewise characterizes life in 'busy, bustling, rushing, hurrying London' as a repulsive and dehumanizing affair, full of 'hungry mouths' (*PP* 48; 80), begins to take on new dimensions, emerging as a record of social chaos and its ensuing social conflicts. Like Marx, Engels and Galton, Stoker takes up an anti-industrialist position. As Jerry, an old-fashioned Irish craftsman rather than an unskilled English 'hand', walks 'bewildered' through the streets searching for work, he keeps thinking 'how different all would have been had he remained at home': 'Here sickness and trouble would have been his surest titles to the help and sympathy of his many friends; but in London, amid strangers, where the maxim of life seems to be "Every man for himself" – all was different, and to be down in the world was to be trampled on.' (*PP* 81)

In this sense, the novel that points us towards the monstrous and the supernatural can also be described as 'realist' in the sense that it gives detailed attention both to individual characters and their environment; that we are presented with largely credible circumstances and events; and that Stoker deals with contemporary social problems. Jerry's experiences are specifically those of a working-class man in London in the 1870s. And one context for *The Primrose Path* is thus the urgency with which mid-nineteenth century writers debated the figure of the alienated worker in a capitalist, free-market economy. Similar scenes are to be found in other Victorian stories of industrial misery – Elizabeth Gaskell's *Mary Barton* (1848) and Charles Dickens' *Hard Times* (1854) are the most famous but there are other stories set specifically in London, notably Andrew Mearns's *The Bitter Cry of Outcast London* (1883) and George Gissing's *The Workers in the Dawn* (1880), written to show the 'ghastly condition...of our poor class....'[18] Like these novels, *The Primrose Path* draws attention to the discrepancies between Britain's 'greatness, wealth and strength' and its 'counterfoils' of 'crime, poverty and disease', at the same time that it anticipates the existential images used by the later generation of modernist writers (*PP* 49). Jerry feels like 'an atom in the midst of the world around him – a grain of sand in that great desert which men call London' (*PP* 50). However, one of the main contradictions of *The Primrose Path* is that, while Stoker writes what seems to be a denunciation of the cruelty of nineteenth-century industrial progress, the novel's surface ideology (formed out of the conventions of temperance fiction) is in no doubt whatsoever that Jerry's well-being is a matter of individual responsibility. In this regard, the novel's presentation of this idea might also usefully be read in relation to such contemporary texts as Samuel Smiles's handbook on self-determination, *Self-Help* (1859). The idea that the male worker might be forced to give up his bodily possession of 'self' through alcohol went against the grain of many of the most fundamental capitalist beliefs, in particular the notion that a progressive market economy was one in which a man's body was his own property, to use or hire out as he wished. As Gretchen Murphy has shown, differences in wealth among individuals were the result of their different abilities to master their bodies and to use them to accumulate capital. The worker who rented his labour to earn a wage was merely disposing of his body as s/he privately chose.[19]

What this comes down to in practice is that *The Primrose Path* follows other contemporary temperance tracts in firstly highlighting the inability of the male drunkard (Jerry) to free himself and secondly emphasizing the necessity of abstinence to liberate working men from intemperance and, by implication, poverty. Jerry loses his economic self-determination and his ability to support his family due to the inadequacies of his own body. He is not a victimized wage slave, but a slave of the bottle and Stoker stresses that the family manage to live relatively comfortably when Jerry is earning and not drinking.[20] One could say, of course, that Jerry is never free and is always ensnared by the capitalist system and its representatives in the form of his exploitative employers. However, according to the logic of the temperance novel, this state of being sober and being 'for hire' is better than being enslaved and Stoker is explicit about the state of dread and powerlessness Jerry's addiction causes. The wages of drunkenness turn out, after all, to be death. The hero's downward spiral, which culminates in poverty, wife-beating, murder, and finally suicide, is made an example to all readers in the novel's final paragraph:

> Jerry walked home on set purpose, and entered the garret where Katey, wearied out of her long waiting, lay asleep in bed. The first things he saw was the tool-basket on the table, beside a bottle and glass....Katey woke with the noise, and the children woke also, and sat up with their little eyes fixed with terror. Jerry went to the bed side and caught Katey's hand. 'Get up' he said....he stooped and picked up a hammer, which had rolled out of the tool-basket.
>
> Katey saw the act and screamed, for she read murder in his eyes. He clutched her by the arm, and raised the hammer; she struggled wildly, but he shook her off, and then, with a glare like that of a wild beast, struck her on the temple.
>
> She fell as if struck by lightning.
>
> When he saw her lying on the floor with the blood streaming around her and forming a pool, the hammer dropped from his hand, and he stood as one struck blind....'Katey, Katey, what have I done? Oh, God, what have I done? I have murdered her. Oh? The drink! The drink! Why didn't I stay at home and this wouldn't have happened?'
>
> He stopped suddenly, and rushing over to the tool basket, took up a chisel, and with one fierce motion drew it across his throat, and fell down beside the body of his wife. (*PP* 104)

In this passage it is tempting to see Stoker (who in many of his novels exploits different popular genres purely for the effect they could produce) combining the shattered domesticity and self-lacerating demonism made available by the dark temperance mode, with the shock tactics used by Dickens at the end of *Oliver Twist*. There are clear echoes here of the scene in which

Bill Sykes murders Nancy. Using a very interesting 'sight' metaphor (Katey reads 'murder in her husband's eyes; he stands as one struck blind') Stoker clearly wants his readers to be able to visualize the action. Yet there is also a strong ideological content in Stoker's fiction that is very much to the fore in passages like this. Stoker presents what for many Victorians would have been a chilling picture: not only a horrible murder but, as Jerry finally realizes, the self-destruction of 'home', that special sanctified place, a refuge from the threats of the external world, and which occupies a key role in what is known as Victorian domestic ideology. In this home the wife occupies a 'privileged' space, as her husband's helpmeet and nurturer of the family, and above all the family's moral guide. As historians Leonore Davidoff and Catherine Hall have shown, this ideology was central to the establishment and maintenance of a bourgeois sense of identity, as well as being held up as a model for the other classes to copy. In this ideology, family and home were the social agencies that would 'civilize' the ambitious cut-throat world of business or at least provide a much-needed calming influence. This 'domestic ideology' had its origins in the 'Puritan belief in the spiritualisation of the household', which manifested itself in the ritual of family prayers. The ideology also had its basis in a view of women as 'dependent' and thus in need of retreat 'away from the dangers of the "world" into the home which they could construct as a moral haven'.[21] The home was no longer seen as combining the complementary world of man and woman but instead as a women's sphere, from which the male breadwinner would be absent for long periods of time. Such developments led to an increased emphasis on the home as a shelter from the perils threatening those who went out into the cut-throat world of work. Writers such as Sarah Ellis, Isabella Beeton and John Ruskin depicted home as a 'vestal temple' ruled over by woman, 'the place of Peace; the shelter, not only from all injury, but from all terror, doubt and division.'[22] In temperance fiction, the drunkard's desires are clearly disruptive of this entire social fabric. The breakdown in familial and social relations presented in *The Primrose Path* – the way in which Jerry and Katey are set against each other – illustrates this. At the halfway point in the novel when the saintly Katey, having 'attended to her household duties' (*PP* 49), waits alone at night for Jerry to return and, hearing him drunkenly staggering up the stairs, is 'afraid to go to the door lest she should see something to horrify her', the text underlines the fact that the domestic space, the home, which has been established as the bedrock of the social order (the foundation of an ideal, ordered society) is being invaded and destroyed.

It is possible to make a number of other connections between Stoker's novel and a range of ideas involving ideas of home, family and women's roles prevalent at the time the novel was published. Amongst women writers, Sarah Ellis produced a large number of best-selling books, which established for her readers the ideals that would best order their lives, in the light of the social and legal restrictions they faced. The home, she argued, was where religious habits and principles were learned and the domestic character of England (and Ireland) formed. Running a home, Ellis pointed out in *The Women of England* (1839) was a vocation which required a wife and mother to abandon self and acquire a 'new nature' devoted to advancing not only the happiness of her male relatives but their spiritual well-being. Other writers of books of advice and conduct manuals – Sarah Lewis and Eliza Warren – suggested that women had a powerful moral authority that could be exercised over husband and children, over whom they had an influence stemming more from example than from actual instruction. This was also a commonplace of mid-Victorian temperance thought. 'What then is the aid that woman can most fitly lend to the noble science of being "temperate in all things?" asked the American temperance campaigner, Lydia Sigourney. 'Not the assumption of masculine energies, not the applause of popular assemblies, but the still, small voice singing at the cradle-side'.[23] Proclaimed as the 'angel in the house' and mythologized in countless definitions of female subjectivity which charged her to preserve the home as a 'temple',[24] a woman was not only a devoted companion to her husband, a loving protector of her children, a competent manager of her household but a counsellor to alcoholics as well.

The concept of a special mission for women makes itself felt in different ways in *The Primrose Path*, a story which, for all its emphasis on a male drunkard, is a woman's story told partly from a woman's perspective. Like the writers of Victorian

41

conduct and temperance literature, Stoker appears to urge his women readers to view themselves, and their daily responsibilities with great seriousness. The narrator's comment: 'If every wife understood the merits which a cheerful home has above all other places in the eyes of an ordinary man, there would be less brutality than there is amongst husbands, and less hardships and suffering amongst wives', together with his exhortation to wives not to argue with their husbands (*PP* 17; 34), seems to come straight out of Sarah Ellis. Yet the novel also appears to question and interrogate these kinds of domesticating tactics. Stoker dramatizes the conflicts and contradictions within women's roles, for example – as some temperance workers were quick to point out – a drunken, abusive man, rendered women and children especially vulnerable; Katey is persecuted in the very space, the home, that is supposed to be both her sanctuary and stronghold. She is subject to 'bitter longing' and, thanks in no small part to her husband's 'obstinacy and cruelty', exists in a state of 'deadly fear' in her own home (*PP* 70).

One of the most noticeable aspects of the novel then, is the way in which overt agreement with the dominant ideological positions – expressed directly by the narrator or in the conformist sentiments adopted by certain characters (notably the teetotaller, Mr Parnell, and Katey herself) – is also undercut by the sympathies generated in the reader. Many nineteenth-century readers, for example, must have considered Katey's attempts 'not to give way to her feelings' (*PP* 76) admirable but ill-advised, while Mr Parnell's rational advice to Katey not to ignore her wifely duties and not to forget 'that you must be your husband's Guardian Angel in case he falls into any temptation' (*PP* 68) appears unfeeling and impractical when set alongside the animal-like violence of Jerry's drunken rages. One problem with giving wives a policing role is that their power, even within the domestic sphere, is circumscribed and limited. Stoker is also extremely perceptive in his analysis – both in the case of Jerry's and Katey's marriage, and in the cynical marriage of Mr Muldoon and Miss M'Anaspie – of the intricate and darker shadings that make up the power dynamics of such relationships. He writes about the irretrievable destruction of married life, rather than using marriage and domesticity as a means of tying up the plot at the end. Through the figure of Jerry, Stoker fictionalizes the revelations put under the spotlight by Frances Power Cobbe in her 1878 article 'Wife Torture in England', that 'men's lack of respect for women, fostered by women's degraded status within the family and prevalent in society at large' – and bolstered by female submission – 'contributed to the burden of violence borne by women both inside and outside the home'.[25] By cleverly showing Jerry's beating of his wife, Stoker also incorporates J. S. Mill's point in *The Subjection of Women* (1867) that, contrary to received opinion, relations between the sexes have their basis in 'absolute power' and 'brutality'.[26] Jerry's lack of respect for the women in his family is explicit; he 'felt a sort of hostile indignation with all who opposed openly or tacitly his determination' (*PP* 36). Most controversially of all perhaps, the novel points to the ambivalence of the fundamental mid-Victorian middle-class feminine ideals of 'good' wife and 'good' mother. Katey is exactly the passive, childlike, open-hearted, innocent, self-sacrificing woman of the mid-Victorian domestic ideal. Yet it is the fact that she adheres so completely to this cultural ideal that makes her unfit for survival in the competitive, urban world. In describing how, starving and weak, the 'brave little woman tried to meet the storm' but is engulfed by it (*PP* 98), Stoker's difficulties in representing Katey's stance convincingly – his difficulty in simply keeping her alive, let alone powerful – are evident. In the Darwinian terms of the novel, Katey, like Jerry, is a representative of an endangered species; although in her case it is not moral inertia but her imprisonment in the period's prescriptions for women that causes the family's extinction.

The picture of London offered in *The Primrose Path* is profoundly pessimistic: the capital is morally and spiritually dead. It is perhaps no surprise that it is in the savagery and brutal indifference of its streets that the voracious blood-sucking energies of the 'creature' Count Dracula and his victim/ helpmate, Lucy Westenra, will make themselves felt in *Dracula*, taking what they want from Hampstead Heath and the Mile End Road; the former wanting to 'absorb as many lives as he can', the latter wanting to satisfy 'an appetite like a cormorant' (*D* 124). Katey O'Sullivan dies starving but virtuous; she will not leave her alcoholic husband, nor will she prostitute herself with the canker-ridden Grinnell. Whilst Katey is imbued with 'wifely devotion' and interested in only one man, Lucy, a self-confessed 'flirt', sleepwalker and, later, nymphomaniac vampire, is more publicly available. Her complaint, 'Why can't they let a girl marry three men, or as many as want her, and save all this trouble' (*D* 91), suggests that she has none of Katey's fastidiousness. Lucy is not against the idea of getting married but she is unwilling to commit herself exclusively to any of her potential husbands.

DRACULA

Dracula is a much more frightening, and also frightened, text than *The Primrose Path*. It is Stoker's first full-length work of supernatural horror fiction and it marks his full transition into a mode of 'fantastic' writing to which he would return at different points in his career, notably in *The Jewel of Seven Stars* (1903) and *The Lair of the White Worm* (1911). It is impossible to comment usefully on the enormous secondary literature which this and other aspects of the novel have solicited, although some important sources are listed in the Bibliography. It *is* possible, though, to begin a discussion of Stoker's most famous novel by comparing it with the neglected first novel we have been discussing and, in particular, by thinking about the differences between the depictions of the female protagonists. Just as the tragedy of the earlier text follows on from Katey's unwillingness either to leave her husband or to seek help from her family and friends, so part of the crisis of *Dracula* comes from Lucy's predisposition to leech onto whatever person is most likely to gratify her need for money and admiration at a particular moment. In this sense, Lucy is the natural successor to Miss M'Anaspie in *The Primrose Path* – a selfish individualist, contemptuous of established authority, set on the greedy pursuit of clothes, jewellery, lovers and husbands. Lucy is, we are told, 'of too sensitive a nature to go through the world without trouble'; she provokes pity, fear and contempt in more-or-less equal parts, but she is also the locus of the text's interest in questions of gender and sexuality. Stoker's depiction of Lucy's decline follows a definite pattern, from over-sensitivity (due to an implied hereditary weakness) through the development of somnambulistic trances with attendant eroticism, to the emergence of a dual existence which hovers between waking and lethargic states and finally to her eventual death – a death that is officially described as 'nervous prostration following the great loss or waste of blood' (*D* 246). In her new life as the Count's help-mate, the 'bloofer lady' who stalks Hampstead Heath, she takes on the role not only of 'fallen' woman but something that the text finds even more disgustingly 'foul', a middle-class woman who is a child abuser: 'With a careless motion, she flung to the ground, callous as a devil, the child that up to now she had clutched strenuously to her breast, growling over it as a dog growls over a bone' (*D* 249).

Where Katey O'Sullivan's tragedy takes place within a cultural framework centred round family and home, that Katey is loyal to and seeks to uphold, Lucy is not so easily controlled and leaves a trail of destruction in her wake. Indeed, Bram Dijkstra cites Lucy as being 'one of those horrible creatures who prey on the central symbol of the future potential of mankind, the child'[27] and therefore the real source of horror in the novel. In this obscene nightmare, Lucy drinks the blood of children in animalistic, even cannibalistic, fashion but also threatens sexual abuse and sexual recruitment since the bite of the vampire also has the quality of contagion or conversion. By 'vamping' the children, the text seems to suggest that Lucy is a threat to the whole future of Western civilization.

Dracula was published in May 1897 at the height of the patriotic celebrations for Queen Victoria's Diamond Jubilee. The novel attracted a good deal of critical attention – both positive and negative – and sold very well. In the summer of that year, *The Bookman* listed it among the most popular books of the season alongside Henryk Sienkiewicz's Roman epic, *Quo Vadis?*, Flora Steel's Indian Mutiny novel *On the Face of the Waters*, K.S. Ranjitisinhji's *The Jubilee Book of Cricket*, Rhoda Broughton's *Dear Faustina* and *The Private Life of Queen Victoria* 'by one of Her Majesty's servants'. Stoker had been working on the novel since 1890 and the care that he evidently took paid off. The *Glasgow Herald* called it 'an Eerie and gruesome tale' but felt that 'it is much the best book he has written. The reader is held with a spell similar to that of Wilkie Collins' *The Moonstone*'.[28] Novels that dealt with the 'un-dead', the vampire who sapped blood, health and strength were not, however, new and Stoker can be seen to be responding to the demands and opportunities of the literary marketplace.[29] As the writer of an article 'The Trail of the Vampire' for the *St James' Gazette* noted: 'There is no more fascinating theme for weird and mysterious fiction than that of the vampire or the werewolf and many admirable stories...have been contrived about these mythical "creatures of the night".[30] For this and many other reviewers, Stoker was simply 'taking in hand', as the *Daily News* termed it, a well-established sub-genre stretching back to John Polidori's *The Vampyre* (1819). Julien Gordon's *Vampires,* which depicted the draining of a young man's energy by his wife and mother-in-law, had been published in 1891, and, in *The Blood of the Vampire* (1897) by Florence Marryat, a 'fat, flabby half-caste', Mrs Brandt, a woman with 'a lust for blood' is defeated by the professional acumen of a brave, middle-class doctor.[31] Other important influences included Mary Braddon, a friend of Stoker's, who in 1896 had published a story of an elderly female vampire 'Good Lady Duncayne', a character who exploits the sinister potential of blood transfusions by draining off the blood of her young female companion. (Braddon described the character in a letter to Stoker as 'humdrum' in comparison to his own 'magnificent' 'bloofer lady'.)[32] There was also the work of the Irish writer, Sheridan Le Fanu, in particular, his 1872 story of female vampirism *Carmilla*. Stoker's own library included Mary Shelley's *Frankenstein*, E. T. A. Hoffman's *Weird Tales*, Lucy Clifford's *The Last Touches*, an edition of *Faustus – his life and death and descent into hell*, as well as Robert Louis Stephenson's *Dr Jekyll and Mr Hyde*.

There were other influences too. Stoker's working notes for the novel reveal the breadth of his researches and in particular his lifelong interest in folklore, the occult and science. He was familiar with Irish tales of the 'un-dead' from an early age, he read Sabine Baring Gould's *Book of Werewolves* (1865) and Emily Gerrard's 'Transylvanian Superstitions' (1885), and Barbara Belford tells us that Stoker 'attended F. H. Meyer's enthusiastic talk on Freud's experiments, at a London meeting of the Psychical Research group that inquired into thought-reading, mesmerism, apparitions and haunted houses.'[33] Stoker refers to Sigmund Freud's associate Jean-Martin Charcot, whose pioneering treatment of hysteria with hypnotism is mooted in *Dracula* by Van Helsing as a way of tracing the progress of Mina's deterioration. The mention of Charcot and later Max Nordau (whose theory of societal degeneration was linked with sexual and gender disturbances expressed in the figure of the so-called 'New Woman' and the decadent) is one technique used by Stoker to give the novel a contemporary resonance whilst concomitantly acknowledging his debt to an older, less obviously urban, Gothic tradition. *Dracula* feeds off a whole range of *fin de siècle* writing – both fiction and non fiction – and culture (including drama and painting), and it can be productive to look at some of the ways in which people such as Charcot, Nordau, Ellen Terry, Henry Irving, all of whom are referred to in the text, influenced Stoker's writing of it.

Although the vampire novel is one context for the case history of Lucy Westenra, it is vampire fiction re-worked in such a way as to engage more generally with developments in *fin de siècle* culture and society. My purpose in the remainder of this discussion is to consider the ways in which, in *Dracula*, Stoker (uniquely and rather oddly placed as an outsider who found himself at the heart of the patriotic British establishment) is able to flag up an uneasy sense of deficit in both 1890s England and Lucy's perception of it. It is possible to argue that some of the most telling scenes in the novel are those where Lucy is shown – sometimes in her own words, sometimes in her behaviour – to be totally lacking in the attributes of middle-class womanhood, let alone be a participant in the British imperial project in the year of Jubilee.

One way of reading *Dracula* is to say that, like a conduct book, the text teaches young women how to behave: in Mina it models proper behaviour, in Lucy and the Count, improper and 'un-English' behaviour. Many of the novel's initial reviewers saw the story in this light, and it is a theme taken up by Rebecca Stott in *The Fabrication of the Late Victorian Femme Fatale*, her historicist study of the *fin de siècle*. Here, Stott shows how Stoker's representation of Lucy, in particular, can be situated within much wider contemporary debates taking place in 1897 – such as the need to 'patrol' and maintain the health of the Empire, and the way in which the moral behaviour of women and their roles as good wives and mothers became matters of increasing concern for all those interested in social purity. Stott draws together different strands of 1890s debate, each of which has been the focus of recent criticism but never so well synthesized by others. The first is the investigation of illicit sexuality; the second the exploration of the themes of invasion, criminality, degeneration and surveillance; and the third is Stoker's own stance as a 'vigilante...of morality'. In contrast to those critics who suggest that *Dracula*'s treatment of the issues of gender and sexuality can be read as indicative of Stoker's own psychological anxieties, Stott posits that Stoker's personal anxieties, which he exhibited not only in his novels but in polemic articles such as 'The Censorship of Fiction' (1908) (discussed in chapter 4), were also shared public ones born out of a 'pervasive sense of moral decline', a sense that the nation was becoming enfeebled and that part of the blame for this could be placed at the door of that gendered national subject known as the 'Englishwoman'.

It is within these contexts that *Dracula*'s own apparently obsessive flagging of female purity (embodied in Mina, 'one of God's women') can be read. In 1897, the fears about the dangers to society caused by an unrestrained (alien) sexuality were acute and Stoker's male characters – Jonathan Harker, Professor Van Helsing, Dr Seward – should be seen as 'investigators and 'inquisitors' whose surveillance of those potentially unruly women, Mina and Lucy, is a necessary part of modern industrial society. As a text, *Dracula* 'stresses vigilance in the search for and treatment of what are seen as the evil and destructive (sexual) energies in human interaction'.[34] Of the two central women characters, it is the sexual pleasure-seeker, Lucy Westenra, who represents excess, exhibiting what Stoker's first readers would, in Stott's words, have recognized as 'all the symptoms of nymphomania...the fallen and insatiable woman who must be held down. She is lustful and voluptuous and absorbs the blood of four men'.[35] Recently, Robert Mighall, in his essay ' "A pestilence which walketh in the darkness": Diagnosing the Victorian Vampire' has drawn further links between the novel and wider cultural discourses. He argues that Stoker's night-marish account of the languid, invalid Lucy reads like a case study in the anti-social practices and enervating consequences of 'onanism' or masturbation, as detailed by nineteenth-century sexology and medical guides and later discussed at length by

Sigmund Freud.[36] Whether the 'ghastly, chalky pale' (*D* 150) of Lucy's languid invalid state would have suggested 'self-abuse' to Stoker's contemporary readers is difficult to ascertain; partly this is because, as Mighall notes, the novel's main medical man, Van Helsing, is too delicate to make inquiries. What *is* true is that by conspicuously consuming blood, money and sex, Lucy, the female vampires and the men whom they ensnare are guilty of a form of economic masturbation, whereby their energies are devoted to pleasure rather than being devoted to the uses for which they were intended (i.e. reproduction and maternity). The dream-like scene in which Jonathan Harker is seen 'in an agony of delightful anticipation', quivering and coy before the three aggressive female vampires, 'feeling in my heart a wicked, burning desire that they would kiss me with those red lips' (*D* 68–70), is one instance of this, as well as being an example of the troubling way in which the novel reverses traditional gender roles; another is the way in which Arthur Holmwood has to be physically restrained twice from contaminating himself by responding to Lucy's wanton sexual advances. This was the kind of 'repulsive' event that alarmed some contemporary reviewers; for instance a writer for the ladies' magazine, *The Gentlewoman*, claimed to have been plunged by the 'debasing' text into 'a terrible nightmare, the horror of which envelopes and at the same time fascinates one so that there is no escape from it.'[37] The novel suggests that such 'Medusa'-like women are loathsome because they deprive the men they ensnare of valuable reserves of energy and blood that could have been used as they intended, i.e. for work. This conflation of the economically productive body with the sexual body is one that Michel Foucault in his influential *The History of Sexuality*, traced to the beginning of the seventeenth century, when sexuality began to be regulated according to a set of economic criteria which were inextricably bound to the body's (re)productivity. Sexual acts which did not lead to births and produce new labourers or consumers (such as masturbation, or same-sex relationships) were labelled 'deviant' and criminalized.[38]

One way of reading *Dracula* then, is to say that the text contributes to the constitution of middle-class subjectivity by promoting (via the techniques of terror) the need to incessantly monitor the self and others. Lucy is finally pacified and saved by the novel's middle-class men in a spectacularly orgiastic scene which, as many critics have noted, 'reads less like salvation than violent sex'[39] (or even rape), exposing in a potentially alarming way the men's primitive nature beneath the veneer of decorum and manners. There is a good deal of puffing and panting and screaming. Though Lucy struggles 'Arthur never faltered...his untrembling arm rose and fell, driving deeper and deeper the mercy-bearing stake, whilst the blood from the pierced heat welled and spurted up around it...the sight gave us courage...And then the writhing and quivering of the body became less....Finally it lay still' (D 254). It is only with the 'witch hunt' and the interrogation mounted by the 'band of light' working together in a tribal reinscription of self-controlled masculine energy that British society can return to normal relations of social exchange. To follow the logic of this argument to its conclusion, what Stott terms, the 'cathartic expulsion' of the Count, and the violent staking (or punishment) of Lucy – which, as Dr Seward somewhat euphemistically puts it, is part of her 'treatment' – are 'acts of high social duty' designed to cleanse the nation.[40] The violent working-over of Lucy releases 'holy calm', 'Lucy, as we had seen her in her life, with her face of unequalled sweetness and purity' (D 255). Of course, one of the several sinister things that strikes a resisting reader is the way in which at the novel's end, Lucy is redeemed by the reinstatement of gender-specific adjectives that diminish her as much as mutilation does: 'sweet', 'calm', 'dear'. These terms re-capture and re-establish Lucy as a naturally compliant and child-like woman, rather than as an energetic and monstrous 'Thing' devoid of gender; the innocent victim (so the men want to believe) of a more powerful external monster. This scene also reminds us of the power dynamics operating in the text through its narrative positioning/focus: for example, Lucy is usually seen before she sees, and seen from a viewpoint which is always trying to reduce her in proportion to those observing her. As a middle-class woman, Lucy's proper role is to 'be' not to 'do' and the text celebrates her being put back in her proper place.

One way of starting a New Historicist critique of a literary text is to quote from another text that offers a brief snapshot of what the critic wants to expand on, in relation to the main work under discussion. Thus in *The Fabrication of the Late Victorian Femme*

Fatale, Rebecca Stott begins her discussion of Stoker with an extract from an article written by the Earl of Dunraven, published in the journal *The Nineteenth Century* in 1892, in which he argues that immigration is harmful to the British nation and results in '[a] paralysing, demoralizing body-and-soul destroying effect upon our people.'[41] Such comments are reminders that as a work of fiction, *Dracula* need not be assumed to have a pedagogical function relating to women's behaviour; it might equally be considered, for example, as a vehicle of the inscription of anxieties about competing 'master' races, about identities and borders more generally. This reading does not exclude or repress *Dracula*'s gendered possibilities but merely shows how in this, as in any literary text, a number of different impulses operate simultaneously and can overlap. At the time of the novel's composition, these anxieties were made more acute in the context of normative conceptions of identity by other malevolent British-based 'undesirables' who seemed to be encroaching on London – Fenians, alcoholics, socialists, the proletariat, spiritualists, Jews and homosexuals. In *Dracula*, the Count, with his terrible odour, his undercover nightly activities, his carrying out of household chores, his long pointed nails, his fondness for dirt naps, and Jonathan Harker's involuntary shudder when the Count touches him, has been seen to stand (allegorically) for all of these outcasts, 'a dream figure of a troubled social group' as David Punter puts it.[42]

> There lay the Count...the mouth was redder than ever, for on the lips were gouts of fresh blood, which trickled from the corners of the mouth and ran over the chin and neck. Even the deep burning eyes seemed set amongst swollen flesh, for the lids and pouches underneath were bloated. It seemed as if the whole awful creature were simply gorged with blood; he lay like a filthy leech exhausted with his repletion. (*D* 83)

Whilst the association of the Count with foreign influence is relevant to contemporary associations of, for example, homosexuality with alien cultures, it also gains a good deal of impetus from the sense that the Count, with his peculiar combination of cosmopolitanism and debased animalism, descended from 'a conquering race' and with a 'lust for power' is a contaminating monstrous 'Other': an un-Christian, Eastern aristocrat transported to democratic England. He invests himself with the advantages of property and a quasi-feudal power over the people he 'vamps'. The Count's mobility becomes in this account both a repressive imposition of upper-class values and a narrative of what Stephen Arata, in a very influential essay, 'The Occidental Tourist' (1990), has termed 'reverse colonization', a sense that 'what has been represented as the civilized world [i.e. England] is on the point of being colonized by primitive forces 'released from bondage.[43] The fact of Stoker's own mixed ethnic heritage, his being like Oscar Wilde, Irish not English-born, has been taken as providing the soil from which this idea sprang; in postcolonial terms, a case of the 'Empire writes back'.[44] But it can also be related to contemporary anxieties about racial superiority and the weakening of British overseas power, a pervasive narrative of the 1890s. This was a period in which one London East End Conservative MP rallied his voters by warning that: 'There is scarcely an Englishman in this room who does not live under the constant danger of being driven from his home, packed out into the streets, not by the natural increase of our population, but by the off-scum of Europe'. Even Sidney Webb's socialist Fabian pamphlet on *The Declining Birth-rate* complained of the danger of 'freely breeding alien immigrants' so that the country would be 'gradually falling to the Irish and the Jews'.[45] Stoker's fiction, designed for a metropolitan audience, is written on the cusp of a change between the unlimited expansionist ethos of Britain's 'New Imperialism' celebrated in Queen Victoria's 'Jubilee of Jubilees', as *Punch* described it,[46] and fears that Britain was losing her power and was being over-run. In Stephen Arata's reading of *Dracula,* the text expresses the colonial master-slave relationship between Britain and its colonies being overturned; in 'the marauding, invasive Other [Dracula], British culture sees its own imperial practices mirrored back in monstrous forms.' As Jonathan Harker predicts, Dracula's supernatural invasion by sea of Whitby is followed by the rapid advance of this horrid, alien, colonizing germ on metropolitan London, and it seems as if the horrors of racial intermingling and cross-breeding that the Count represents are to be realised there. Harker's revulsion is acute: 'This was the being I was helping to transfer to London, where, perhaps, for centuries to come he might, amongst its teeming millions, satiate his lust for blood, and create a new and ever-widening circle of semi-demons to batten on the helpless' (*D* 84). Later, the sight of the Count trolling down to his new house in Piccadilly – one of London's prime arterial routes, as well being one of the haunts of rent-boys and prostitutes – prompts the nervous Harker to suffer a 'relapse.'

This all-encompassing fear of 'Others', and especially of a foreign, aristocratic predator with designs on 'your great England' as the Count puts it (*D* 50), is one reason for the text's obsession with surveillance – the possibility of sighting but also the possibility of being deceived by someone's appearance which may only be the semblance of reality. Stoker's own interest in the difficulties of finding out what people are 'like' makes itself felt throughout his fiction from *The Primrose Path* to the *Lair of the White Worm*. It also resurfaces in his non-fictional work, notably in *Famous Impostors* (1910), a study of 'impersonators, pretenders, swindlers and humbugs of all kinds; those who have masqueraded in order to acquire wealth, position, or fame' (*FI* v). In *Dracula*, a novel preoccupied with doubling, betrayal, 'pretending' and imagining' on all kinds of physical and psychological levels, it is the 'fallen-woman' Lucy's convincing turn as the 'nicely dressed' bloofer lady that, aided by her innate cunning and her harmless appearance, as Leslie Ann Minot has shown, enables her to lure the children away. Likewise, in Transylvania, role-play is also central to the Count's plans for mastery; he dresses in Harker's clothes in order to kidnap a child for the three vampire women to feast on and makes sure that if Harker manages to escape he will not be welcome in the district. The female vampires who approach Harker also appear 'by their dress and manner' to be 'ladies', though by their behaviour they reveal themselves to be nothing of the sort. What is seen is invariably a façade: Dr Van Helsing's rebuke to Dr Seward – 'You do not let your eyes see nor your ears hear' (*D* 228) encapsulates the text's preoccupation with the need for, and disciplinary power of, the clinical gaze. As Minot argues, 'if people are not what they seem, they lose their meaning and suggest, in a quite alarming way, possible changes in the order of things.'[47] Minot goes on to note that one reason why the Count presents such an insidious threat is because he is able to make himself blend in. On his visit to England he wishes to avoid being 'a stranger in the stranger land' and announces: 'did I move and speak in your London, none there are who would not know me for a stranger. That is not enough for me...I am content if I am like the rest, so that no man stops if he sees me, or pause in his speaking if he hear my words, to say, "Ha, ha! A stranger!"' (D 51)

As part of his sinister homework, the Count, as Vesna Goldsworthy has noted, keeps some very unexpected volumes in his 'vast' library in the castle.[48] It contains a London directory, *Whittaker's Almanac* detailing national events, magazines, and even *Bradshaw* and British railway timetables. In preparation for his visit to England, the Count studies these publications in detail and through them he tells Jonathan, he has come 'to know your great England, and to know her is to love her' (D 50). Understanding the English gives him the power to colonize their women, or even worse, their men, invasively through 'filthy' 'un-English' sexual practices, turning them into clones of himself: 'My revenge has just begun! I spread it over centuries and time is on my side. Your girls that you all love are mine already; and through them you and others shall yet be mine' (D 317). The Count's words are ominous because they suggest that although elderly and effeminate, he is also a fantasy stereotype of enhanced masculinity who confronts the native Englishman with his own sexual inadequacy, suggesting the even more horrendous possibility that a generation of women are looking elsewhere for sexual satisfaction. This is another reason why the Count is so dangerous: as a foreign import he cannot be readily banished through the reassertion of a patriotic fervour seen to occur naturally in the year of the Jubilee. Whilst Stoker suggests that the patriot (masculine) is a stronghold of British values and a powerful antidote to the blood-sucking contagion of the Count, the bored, leisured English woman is liable to go over to the other side – she may even be the enemy of little English children, like Lucy Westenra, who at night invites the Count to feed on her by deliberately pulling the garlic away from her throat. This is why, it is often suggested, that in the logic of the text, women require surveillance because they are by nature unruly and disloyal, subject to continuous internal rebellion fermented by their reproductive systems. Even Mina announces, of her own experience of being forced to suck the blood from the

Count's chest, 'I did not want to hinder him', although, unlike Lucy, she remains loyal to the idea of the 'proper lady', is not sexually excited and understands it as a kind of betrayal that makes her 'unclean' (D 327; 326). The text's distinction between patriots and women (the former rejecting the Count, the latter embracing him and his nasty atavistic aristocratic values) is one of the things that the novel struggles to come to terms with, and to which Stoker, in a manner which often embarrasses his readers, responds with a powerful, often bizarre mix of racist assertion and misogynistic anxiety. So it is that the narrative moves inexorably towards Lucy's staking and decapitation, and the subsequent imposition of sentimental discourse on her dead body – a blood-splattered re-colonization of conquered territory and brutal shaping of women into English national subjects.

In the final stages of the novel, the text tries to be dismissive of the Count – a phantom would-be Englishman – by stressing the gulf between the evil, 'deathly pale', effete old Transylvanian un-dead with his 'horrible vindictive look', and the hypermasculine English and American living heroes, described as 'earnest', 'chivalrous', 'brave', 'true'. This culminates in the desperate chase back to Transylvania, the ripping open of the Count's coffin and the 'miracle' of his destruction. As Harker's kukri (symbolic of British imperial power) 'shears through the throat' and Quincy Morris's bowie knife (the weapon of American pioneers) plunges 'in the heart', 'the whole body crumbles into dust' (D 417–18).

The text begins to take on new dimensions; emerging as a record of social crisis but, infused with nationalism, it also suggests ways of managing this same crisis. It flags up the 'scientific chastity' of Van Helsing's scientific knowledge and male heroism, whilst reproducing a sentimental discourse upon Mina who, like Katey O' Sullivan in *The Primrose Path*, becomes the embodiment of the 'Good' woman: passive, decorous, nurturing, obedient yet resilient, and capable of the internal surveillance, which according to Michel Foucault is what distinguishes the modern middle-class subject. As a modern woman, Mina (unlike Katey) becomes the bridge between private and public spheres. One might even say that the large (phallic) revolver Mina wields in the final battle (but does not use) represents feminine maternal power both liberalized and

55

externalized. Yet whilst the text, with its (middle) class and nation-building intent, seems emphatic that there is a system of values that is authentic and viable – one that is not concerned with greed – accepting these values whole-heartedly has tended to raise some difficult questions for modern readers.

Whilst the journey of the novel's male heroes involves travelling onward and upwards through the world, eventually reaching psychological and financial autonomy, the route of the female hero's (Mina's) life is, like that of many other nineteenth-century female *bildungsromans*, something of a dead-end. The limitations placed on women are difficult to throw off and as Mina says, represent 'a bitter pill for me to swallow.' One of the reasons why feminist critics have tended to find the text worthy of attention is because of the way in which, in his presentation of Mina, Stoker reveals the conflicts between these possibilities of growth, between what a new emphasis on the idea of individuality might offer women (via forms of education and career, for example) and what was considered the proper structure of a woman's life: a life, that is, without incident. In the early sections of the novel, Mina, brimming with energetic potential, 'overwhelmed with work', and with a 'man's brain', goes out into the public world, maps out the plan of attack on the Count and thereby takes control of the text's narrative. Yet, as the men come to believe that Mina and Lucy have actually got quite a lot in common with the female vampires, the two women are ushered into a diminishing space (literal and metaphorical) and Mina's possibilities for action suppressed on medical grounds. Dr Seward observes 'it is no place for a woman, and if she had remained in touch with the affair it would in time infallibly have wrecked her' (*D* 295). Although she is later re-admitted to the male group by offering hypnosis as a way of tracking the Count down, the juxtaposition of Mina's thwarted energy with the rather dull passivity of Lucy emphasizes just how convention has curtailed Mina's aspirations toward participation and development. Mina lacks her husband's easy mobility and she is effectively silenced as the men try to reassert traditional gender boundaries. Knowing that 'the blood is the life', Van Helsing is relieved to find Mina looking 'thin and pale and weak' when he returns to her after Lucy's staking, that is to say, like the picture of the delicate

Victorian lady. 'I was glad to see her paleness and her illness, for my mind was full of the fresh horror of that ruddy Vampire sleep.' Ultimately, Stoker is forced to satisfy the demand for narrative closure in a cloying flood of self-sacrifice, motherhood and silence, 'sweetness and loving care'. Once Mina is unable to articulate her own experiences, she is no longer able, with colonial intent, to attempt to appropriate the men's adventure narrative. The final words of the novel let us know that there is nothing better than this, that there is no other way of being that gives a woman as much dignity as being a quiet wife and mother, certainly not the noisy relentless quest for material and carnal satisfaction followed by Lucy Westenra. The text's narrative discontinuities ensure that it is hard not to feel that, as a result of her entrapment within the domestic sphere, Mina escapes one kind of victimization only to tumble into another. Stoker gives credit to Mina for her willingness to play her role, her realization, for instance, that to become part of society you have to go along with it. He also hints that Lucy's restless acquisitiveness is the future: her actions – distasteful though they seem – open the possibilities for women in the future.

THE JEWEL OF SEVEN STARS

If *Dracula* is generally understood to be the greatest of Stoker's novels, *The Jewel of Seven Stars* at least matches it in its complexity, scale and scope and, like *Dracula,* succeeds in being at once satisfyingly straightforward while generating a variety of enigmas, connotations and questions. It is like *Dracula* in several respects. Again it is set in London, and again, like *The Primrose Path* and *Dracula,* it can be inserted into a number of different interpretative frames and its generic identity discussed in various ways. Like *Dracula,* it is a text which exploits the craze for fictional invasion narratives which had begun with George Chesney's *The Battle of Dorking* (1871), continued through H. G. Wells's *The War of the Worlds* (1897) and reached a culmination in Arthur Conan Doyle's *The Poison Belt* (1913), all of which present the nightmare vision of the conquest of Britain. *The Jewel of Seven Stars* is also a mummy novel grounded in the form of the Gothic, with its nightmare vision of the home. Stoker uses the Gothic's associations with what is 'other, subversive and marginal, and thus the site of ambivalence', in Tamar Heller's words, to construct a story about female criminality and victimization but one which, like *Dracula*, is located in a historical reality with particular implications for women.[49] And yet, whilst *The Jewel of Seven Stars* is interested in describing women's roles in society, there is a man at its centre, through whom the events of the novel are related. Malcolm Ross QC is a young barrister, more worldly than Jonathan Harker but with a similar mind-set. An intelligent and confident man, who prides himself on his skills of observation which 'extend[s] to my life outside as well as within the courthouse', Ross seems a suitable figure to whom to entrust a fantastical story of the occult and the supernatural as it impinges upon modern London. He is the new 'modern citizen' as described by Ronald Thomas in *The Cambridge Companion to the Victorian Novel* in his account of mid-Victorian detective fiction and the work of Wilkie Collins.[50] He is, like Stoker, a member of the 'privileged professional elite'; the man of science, engineering or law who had replaced the clergyman as the source of moral counsel and advice. Malcolm Ross's generation stands on the cusp of two very different epochs – the novel was published in 1903, two years after the accession of King Edward VII, but is set at the end of the reign of Queen Victoria – and Ross himself is caught between the two. He is socially enlightened and forward-looking but he is also an adherent to older codes of English behaviour.

The story of *The Jewel of Seven Stars* begins when Ross is woken in the middle of the night by a knock on his door and summoned to the house of a young woman he has recently met, as an attempt has been made on her father's life. He is already deeply in love with Margaret Trelawny and is dreaming of her when the knock comes. Abel Trelawny has been found lying unconscious beside his safe, having been dragged bleeding from his bed. The safe has not been opened, and there are no signs of forced entry. The doctors are baffled but Ross suspects a connection between the attack and the extraordinary collection of Egyptian relics that fills the house. It emerges that twenty years before, whilst excavating the ancient tomb of Queen Tera, a woman of 'extraordinary character', Trelawny, an archaeologist, fell into a three-day trance in the Mummy pit. During this unconscious period his wife back home died giving birth to Margaret who, in the meantime, has grown into the dead Queen's double. Trelawny's research is leading up to 'The Great Experiment' – the reanimation of Queen Tera.

The result, as the *Review of Reviews* noted disapprovingly in 1903, is 'an extraordinary story....Those who like the weird and the uncanny, a mixture of black magic with a dash of spiritualism, astral bodies of ancient Egyptian mummies committing assaults which baffle specialists and London detectives of symbolism and mystery, of the inexplicable and unexplained of every kind, will curdle their blood and possibly addle their brains over this mystifying medley of ancient Egypt and the twentieth century of the Christian Era'.[51]

As these reactions suggest, this is another text in which Stoker is interested in clashes between past and present and also between cultures – West/East, Christian/pagan, science/occult-ism. As David Seed points out in his excellent essay 'Eruptions of the Primitive into the Present', the text is also another invasion narrative concerned with the way in which a primitive, foreign, apparently conquered culture 'imposes its presence on Stoker's contemporary world' and in doing so 'bring[s]...into question characters' assumptions about the nature and stability of their reality'.[52] London's well-being derives, as the *Review of Reviews* noted in its discussion of the novel in 1903, from 'specialists and London detectives' and from technological advances; the text is 'saturated' with references to new discoveries such as Röntagen's new 'forces of light' (X-rays) which can, it is asserted, be utilized to explain the dark forces of ancient Egyptian magic.[53] Yet, whilst Mr Trelawny talks about mankind entering into a new scientific age, having reached 'that stage of intellectual progress in which the rough machinery for making discovery is being invented', it is plain that the gap produced by such knowledge – which seems to give the civilized modern world the upper hand over the unruly ancient one – is illusory: the malevolent astral body in the Egyptian tomb can come back to life, free to make a move anywhere and on any one. For modern civilized London, such malevolent traces or 'remains' of the past, as Nicholas Royle has described them, are not just irritants, 'the remains of something that was once present' they are that which, in being spectral, prevents 'any present, and any experience of the present from being completely itself.' This spectre from the past has the ability to interrupt not only the present moment but also any sense of identity. It takes Trelawny's daughter, Margaret, the representative of pure English womanhood, to shock Malcolm Ross into recognizing that what is at stake is not only his country and his class but his personal interest in the woman he loves: 'the resurrection of woman and the woman's life' (*JSS* 182). It is Margaret Trelawny who is able to make him see the alternative: 'the abandonment of your Familiar to death – to annihilation'. (*JSS* 195)

The craze for Egyptology took off in Victorian literature and culture from the 1880s, the main focus being, according to Richard Pearson, a 'fascination with the *un*dead of antiquity', the linking of sexual desire and death and the cultural clashes between Modern and Ancient worlds.[54] Arthur Conan Doyle, whom Stoker remembered in his *Personal Reminiscences* as a close friend, wrote an archaeological thriller 'The Ring of Thoth' (1890) which makes great play of the juxtaposition between pagan, Christian and scientific beliefs, as well as making the most of the erotic arousal inherent in the act of exhumation and the acquisitiveness which formed the cornerstone of late-Victorian archaeology. Stoker exploits this version of popular Egyptology; he describes men who are captivated by, but also dismissive of, the Egyptian past. The vulture-like Corbeck, Trelawny's assistant, who moves between ancient Egypt and modern London and makes 'a living of a sort' by 'tomb hunting', is used by Stoker to cast an embarrassed eye on the behaviour of English archaeologists abroad:

> 'I have been several times out on expeditions in Egypt for your father...Many of his treasures – and he has some rare ones, I tell you – he has procured through me, either by my exploration or by purchase – or – or – otherwise. Your Father...He sometimes makes up his mind that he wants to find a particular thing...and he will follow it all over the world until he gets it'. (*JSS* 69)

There is some sense of (male) loyalty between employer and employee in this account but no cultural or human sensitivity of the kind Margaret displays in her horror at the unveiling of the mummified Queen Tera: '"A woman is a woman, if she had been dead five thousand centuries!"' The main point of Stoker's critique of Egyptology – as expressed in Trelawny's response '"Not a woman, dear; a mummy!"' (*JSS* 199) – is to offer a striking reminder of the closeness between archaeology and grave-robbing. It also highlights the colonial intent of the West toward the Orient, which (as Nicholas Daly has noted) involves 'the objectification not merely of its cultures, but of its peoples'.[55] The ethics of archaeology were, of course, different then from what they are now, but Stoker makes it fairly clear that viewing the Trelawny's Notting Hill house stashed with booty – where 'so many strange relics are on view...that unconsciously one was taken back to strange lands and strange times' – is an eerie but also a diminishing experience. The appreciation of beauty and artefact has become a debased and dangerous form of possession. The house could simply be the British Museum rather than a domestic space. Yet, as Daly has pointed out, whilst the role of the Museum was to impose order on the deluge of exotic artefacts brought back into Britain, even the novel's modern man of science, the doctor Sir James Frere, is in no doubt that there is a link between Trelawny's coma and the house's 'assemblage of horrors' and its maze of locked doors and darkened passages (*JSS* 49).[56]

Stoker was fond of secret mansions and underground passageways and his characters invariably have some kind of subterranean existence. Keeping vigil over Mr Trelawny in an over-furnished bedroom stuffed full of curios, Malcolm Ross feels as if he has been incarcerated or buried alive, cut off from the bustling London streets, able to hear only 'the occasional roll of wheels, the shout of a reveller, the far-away echo of whistles and the rumbling of trains' (*JSS* 32). Although he feels inspired by a sense that his devotion to Margaret has 'brought out all the masculinity in me' (*JSS* 206) he is also aware, in this hothouse of occultism, of something else working 'on my nerves – on my memory – on my very will' (*JSS* 31) and, conscious of the need to control this growing hysteria, he tries to take refuge in 'a world of facts': 'These scientific discussions (regarding the experiment) soothed me: they took my mind from brooding on the mysteries of the occult' (*JSS* 32). Ultimately, however, each time Ross thinks he has gained mastery over his feelings, he finds himself in some other dark passage of the mind. It is 'some other thought, darker and deeper' lying behind what can be seen, 'one whose voice had not found him as yet' (*JSS* 53) that haunts him once the date of the Great Experiment approaches. As the designated evening draws near, so Margaret becomes more and more aloof and reserved. On one level, Margaret, like the other Egyptian jewels, disappears. Ross observes her strange silence, her withdrawal into herself, her strange mood swings: she becomes the puzzle to be solved, and brought back to her normal place. On another level, and in keeping with the novel's plot, the task, as Laurence Rickels notes, is not so much detective work as excavation. Rickels observes similarities between the search for Margaret (described in Stoker's text of 1903) and another great early twentieth-century experiment – the auto-analysis that Sigmund Freud always compared to archaeological excavation. In the novel this 'comes full circle in the person of Margaret wired to [the] Mummy's dictation'. Malcolm Ross records how: 'I was beginning to doubt Margaret!...Margaret was changing....It was almost as if she were speaking parrot-like or at dictation of one who could read words or acts, but not thoughts' (*JSS* 34–5).[57] With each 'mysterious veiling of her own personality', the narrator registers a 'subtle sense of separation' and he begins to be 'afraid of her' (*JSS* 36; 82).

Like *Dracula*, the text also plays on Freud's sense of the uncanny (*das unheimliche*), that set of frightening experiences installed within, or arising out of familiar surroundings. Malcolm Ross's strange experience resonates with Martin Heidigger's description of the *unheimlich* as 'that which casts us out of the "homely" i.e. the customary, secure'.[58] Ross's quest turns out to be a quest for identity, both his own and Margaret's. His task produces a crisis of personal identity but it also involves him plumbing the 'mysterious depth[s]' (*JSS* 30) of his own and Margaret's lives.

Margaret Trelawny, as Malcolm Ross's narration sees things, is at the centre of this story about possession and possessions. She is 'the young girl' initially seen in Ross's dream, sheltered from 'the great world with its disturbing trouble, and its more disturbing joys' (*JSS* 5). The jagged knife wounds that appear on Mr Trelawny disrupt the household and set in motion the turmoil around which the plot is constructed, but it is

Margaret's behaviour (and the male character's unravelling of that behaviour) that keeps the plot moving. In Margaret the reader is introduced once again to the 'strange dual existence' that we saw in Lucy Westenra:

> Miss Trelawny met me in the hall. She was not in any way shy. She seemed to rule all around her with a sort of high-bred dominance, all the more remarkable as she was greatly agitated and as pale as snow. In the great hall were several servants, the men standing together near the hall door, and women clinging together in the further corners and doorways. A police superintendent had been talking to Miss Trelawny...As she took my hand impulsively there was a look of relief in her eyes, and she gave a gentle sigh of relief. Her salutation was simple.'I knew you would come.' (*JSS* 8)

The language used in this scene sheds interesting light on Malcolm Ross's (and indeed Stoker's) concern not only with a crisis in the middle-class household but with larger issues of class and gender. Though by the end of the nineteenth century the position of women had begun to change – in 1894 *The Quarterly Review* noted that 'women are now graduates in half a dozen professions and disciples in all' – the ideology of Stoker's heroes moves at a much slower pace.[59] Ross, for instance, admires Margaret's unstinting devotion to her father (who is clearly an inadequate parent) and her management of the household, and he wants to regard her very much as a model woman – in terms reminiscent of those to be found in John Ruskin's 'Of Queen's Gardens' (1865) which, with its emphasis on the home as a 'temple', had helped elevate Victorian married love half a century earlier.[60] Ross writes of Margaret that 'The whole harmony of her being seemed complete'; hers was 'a personality that dominated either by its grace, its sweetness; its beauty, or its charm' (*JSS* 22). As he notes approvingly, Margaret's life with her father has left her 'naïve and unconscious; so girlish and simple' (*JSS* 21) and seemingly dependent on men like himself ('she took my hand impulsively'). As well as responding as an English gentleman to those aspects of Margaret's appearance that signify her status as a lady, Ross also resents the invasion of the middle-class household, defined as we have seen, as a predominantly female space, by what he assumes to be uncouth lower-class policemen.

Monitoring women, Ross, thinks, is his own task, not only because he can understand middle-class femininity better than the policemen, but also because it is a means to an end; a way of proving himself after the fashion of the hero of adventure romance, worthy of the woman's love.

Whilst Margaret is interpreted in consistently sentimentalizing terms, the text also exploits fears about the fluidity of middle-class female identity.[61] For what Ross also sees, but does not wish to believe, is that Margaret's identity is in the middle of a process of splitting; 'under the shadow of another form' she is transformed into the 'marvellously strong' (but less feminine) woman whose 'energy [is] manifest in every nerve and fibre of her being'. Self-control, independence, intelligence, physical strength, the desire to make up her own mind – those signs of Margaret's attractiveness are also the traces of Queen Tera who 'had won secrets from nature in strange ways, and had 'claimed all the privilege of kingship and masculinity'. They are also the stereotypical signs of an equally feared, but more modern, 1900s counterpart: the ambitious 'New Woman' and the 'Wild Woman' – the latter characterized at the time by Eliza Lynn Linton as 'a woman who does anything specially unfeminine and ugly'[62] – and the suffragette. Read alongside these contexts, Margaret's materialization as Queen Tera is not just a trapping of the 'uncanny'. Instead it is an instance of how in the Gothic novel 'materialization', as Adriana Cracuin (drawing on the feminist theorist, Judith Butler's term from *Bodies that Matter*), demonstrates, 'is inseparable from issues of power and how one (or in what form of woman, one) can exercise more of it'.[63] So, in constantly referring to Queen Tera's lust for power, we might say that Stoker is offering his readers a version of femininity that seems to be undermining the artificial boundaries which Edwardian gender lore sets up between men and women. For late-Victorian writers, both of fiction and non-fiction, the Egyptian mummy plot was very often a way of displacing their sense of unease about the problems of modern womanhood and the long-held ideals of feminine subjectivity that seemed to be under attack. Ross's observation of Margaret that 'Her eyes blazed, and her mouth took a hard, cruel tension which was new to me' (*JSS* 173) is an instance of how the anxieties noted in *Dracula* are again writ large. Stoker's representation of Margaret is full of the contradictions and fears inherent in *fin de siècle* discourses on femininity and the 'Woman Question'. Because Stoker makes considerable use of complementary doubles, his *femmes fatales* can easily be dismissed as nothing more than misogynist stereotypes. But in *The Jewel of Seven Stars*, Stoker's heroine(s) subvert the dominant category of the 'womanly' woman not only by embodying its antithesis but also by demonstrating the instability of the categories themselves. Although they are perceived as 'disturbing' and make Ross 'afraid of her', Margaret's 'queenly' demeanour and ability 'to rule all around her', daughterly devotion (to 'mummy' as well as to daddy, as Rickels wittily notes[64]), plus the fact that she is has 'so little thought of self' and is 'hardly an individual at all but simply a phase of Queen Tera' (*JSS* 78), are in one sense only versions of the loyalty, self-abnegation and daughterly devotion set down by the likes of John Ruskin and Sarah Ellis, and seen as integral attributes of proper femininity.

In *The Jewel of Seven Stars* Stoker's representation of Margaret thus taps into contemporary conceptions about middle-class women generally, relying on a patriarchal framework that is common in many late-Victorian and Edwardian texts. But the recognizability of his literary characters also depends on their basis in particular narrative conventions of plot and genre, and in their similarity to characters in other fictions. Queen Tera, for example, seems to be a distant relative of Ayesha, the tyrannical (anti)heroine of Rider Haggard's 1886 bestseller *She*. Stoker also includes a number of sensational scenes associated with the current craze for Egyptology. The most spectacular of these is Ross's description of the unwrapping of the mummy (Queen Tera again) in the tomb, an act which, as in other mummy novels, gives narrator and characters exotic license, at the same time as it implicates them as participants in a kind of symbolic licensed peepshow:

> The mummy was both long and broad and high; and was of such weight that it was no easy task, even for the four of us to lift it out. Under Mr Trelawny's direction we laid it out on the table prepared for it....Then the work began. The unrolling of the mummy cat had prepared me somewhat for it; but this was so much larger, and so infinitely more elaborate, that it seemed a different thing....But there were the same surroundings, the same attendant red dust and

pungent presence of bitumen; there was the same sound of rending which marked the tearing away of the bandages....As the men unrolled them, I grew more and more excited. I did not take part in it myself; Margaret looked at me gratefully as I drew back....As the unrolling went on, the wrappings became finer, and the smell less laden with bitumen, but more pungent....At last we knew that the wrappings were coming to an end. Already the proportions were reduced to those of a normal figure of the manifest height of the queen, who was more than average tall....We all stood awed at the beauty of the figure which, save for the face cloth, now lay completely nude before us. Mr Trelawny bent over and with hands that trembled slightly, raised this linen cloth which was of the same fineness as the robe. As he stood back and the whole glorious beauty of the Queen was revealed, I felt a rush of shame sweep over me. It was not right that we should be there, gazing with reverent eyes on such unclad beauty. It was indecent; it was almost sacrilegious. And yet the wonder of that beautiful form was something to dream of. (*JSS* 201–2)

Discussing the importance of this type of scene in mummy fiction, David Seed suggests that it should be understood as a transgressive piece of writing, a way by which novelists tried to circumvent the stringent codes of decency operating in the market for popular fiction: 'The exoticism of the erotic project licenses a degree of explicit description difficult to imagine in the context of mainstream novels'.[65] One could also say, however, that within the codes operating in the novel, the scene is not transgressive at all; that the mummified body/ double, whose violation horrifies and entertains, is that of a woman merely confirms what we already know about the male imagination that informs the novel. Under Ross's male gaze, the mummy is a highly-sexualized being and the reader is invited to identify with and join the men in the excitement of unwrapping her, to direct his/her own gaze at the mummy and then to imagine the 'nude' body under the bandages. The unwrapping and vivisection of Queen Tera that the men perform is undertaken in the name of science, but it is also conducted to a significant extent on the level of punishment. Queen Tera violates the 'natural' difference between the sexes and her once-sacred body is laid bare to be violated. The ancient trappings of a powerful femininity are nothing compared to the trappings of a modern, powerful masculinity. The earlier phase in which powerful men like Mr Trelawny have become helpless and feminized is just that – a phase. The men get over it and re-assert their control. As in a similar scene in *Dracula* involving the staking of Lucy Westenra, there is an almost unquestioning acceptance of the malleability that is often ascribed to women's bodies – after death in this instance. At the same time, the construction whereby the dead, sex and the living are linked is apparent in Margaret's objections to the men's unwrapping of the body. By this stage, Margaret has been symbolically identified with the mummy to the extent that she sees the scene as an indecent exposure of herself to the voyeuristic gaze of the male 'experimenters', and there is a very powerful sense that Margaret must be careful that the predatory male group – whether in the name of scientific experiment or self-interest – does not turn on her, another domestic object. In this respect, Stoker's novel matches very neatly Richard Pearson's observation that the symbolic 'unwrappings' that repeatedly appear in mummy novels eventually have the effect of creating 'a complicated inter-relationship between archaeology and sexual perversity, at the same time that they suggest that this kind of violation is nothing special.'[66] In *The Jewel of Seven Stars* such repetitions certainly seem to bear out Pearson's point, particu-larly when we begin to think about the way in which different kinds of writing begin to merge, with detailed realism taking on the qualities of the Gothic and vice versa.

The conclusion of this narrative is not (like most Victorian and Edwardian novels) marriage, but death. The 'Great Experiment' succeeds but all the characters except the narrator are killed when the crypt fills with thick smoke. The blurring of Margaret/Queen Tera (and the none-too subtle suggestion about a woman's explosive sexuality) culminates when Ross realizes that in his confusion he has carried the Egyptian queen to safety, thinking she was Margaret. He puts on a respirator mask and returns to the chamber and finds himself struck by 'a terror which has no name': Margaret is lying on the floor 'gazing upwards with fixed eyes if unspeakable terror...her hands before her face' and with a 'glassy stare' between her fingers 'more terrible than an open glare' (*JSS* 211). The narrative then has to convince the reader that things are returning to 'normal'. ('The storm was dying away as quickly as it had risen and now it only came in desultory puffs' (*JSS* 211)). However the narrator cannot shake off the sense of the high costs paid by women as modernization unfolds. (The revised ending, inserted in the 1912 version of the novel, plays down this demonstration of the sacrifices made by Edwardian womanhood by having Ross rescue and then marry Margaret). The ending of *The Jewel of Seven Stars* makes for uncomfortable reading, for whilst it foregrounds the heroine's (Pyrrhic) victory, the shocking revelation that she has escaped from the confinement of the prison-house only by submitting herself to be murdered is a chilling one. The possibilities of romantic love give a tragic dimension to Trelawny's experiment, and Ross has to play a high price for his commitment to the scientific cause.

The Jewel of Seven Stars is, in many ways, a text that brings together several strains of Stoker's work. Stoker, whether he was writing a short story, novella, or full-length novel, wanted, he claimed, to 'convey abstract ideas of controlling forces and purposes; of thwarting passions; of embarrassing weaknesses; of all the bundle of inconsistencies which make up an item of concrete humanity' (*PR* I x). Yet he sought to do this in a way that would allow him to respond to the demands and opportunities of the marketplace. He wrote within the genres of Gothic fantasy and the occult at various points in his career – at the beginning in the short story collection *Under the Sunset* (1882), in the middle in *Dracula*, *The Mystery of Sea*, *The Jewel of Seven Stars* and at the end in *The Lair of the White Worm* (1911). He used the forms of the fantastic and the occult to unsettle readers' sense of life as they knew it by questioning modern methods and to reveal primitive impulses ('Old Forces which seemed to be coming into contact with the New Civilization' (*JSS* 158) in modern London life and consciousness. In the chapter leading up to the 'Great Experiment', Malcolm Ross wonders: 'Was there room in the Universe for opposing Gods; or if such there were, would the stronger allow manifestations of power on the part of the opposing Force which would tend to the weakening of his own teaching and designs? Surely if this supposition were correct there would be some strange and awful development – something unexpected and unpredictable...' (*JSS* 159). The reader is forced to think about the persistence of the supernatural past in the secular urban present and the vulnerability of modern life in the horrible face of primitive, unpredictable, disordered forces and in *The Jewel of Seven Stars*, Stoker exploits these ideas to the full. He also, of course, suggests that these forces can be overcome if modern men stir themselves into action. As we shall see in the next chapter, Stoker's preoccupation with finding appropriate models of masculinity becomes a recurrent one in his works.

3

Men and Monsters

Throughout his career, Bram Stoker was an energetic writer of adventure romances; his early novella *Buried Treasures*, first serialized – like *The Primrose Path* – in *The Shamrock* (March 1875) has a pair of male friends exploring sunken ships for missing treasure; *The Watter's Mou* (1895) is a tale of smuggling and self-sacrifice in a remote Scottish fishing village; *The Mystery of the Sea* (1903) has the same location plus buried treasure, kidnapping and a cross-dressing heroine who is a descendent of Sir Francis Drake; and the last published novel *The Lair of the White Worm* (1911) is also an adventure novel in which the hero does battle with a deadly serpent-woman. Stoker's use of the forms of the adventure romance and the quest narrative, in which a young man journeys out into the world to accomplish some great feat or to overcome some unspeakable evil, also makes itself felt in many other works, including *Dracula* and *The Jewel of Seven Stars*.

In using the framework of the adventure story, Stoker was trying to exploit what had become an enormously popular (and potentially lucrative) sub-genre of fiction. Two bestsellers – Robert Louis Stevenson's *Treasure Island* (1883) and H. Rider Haggard's *King Solomon's Mines* (1886) – had helped to set in motion a revival of this kind of writing in which, as Stevenson explained in 'A Gossip on Romance' (1882), 'the interest turns, not upon what a man shall choose to do, but how he manages to do it; not on the passionate slips and hesitations of the conscience, but on the problems of the body and of the practical intelligence, in clean open-air adventure...'.[1] Writers such as R. M. Ballantyne, G. A. Henty and W. H. Kingston were recognized, alongside Haggard and Stevenson, as the main romance writers, and they came to be joined from time to time by others such as Marie Louise de la Ramée (who used the pen-name 'Ouida'), Rudyard Kipling, Anthony Hope and John Buchan.[2]

Summarizing the characteristics of the adventure romance or 'imperial romance' (as it is sometimes termed), Deirdre David notes the form's emphasis on 'English national and masculine subjectivity', 'tropes of travel and hazardous adventure' and 'racism [which]...is unembarrassed and extreme' with race as a 'glamorous or demonic marker'.[3] Invariably the main emphasis is on an exciting plot, constructed around a virile (white) hero's adventures in far-flung exotic places, usually Africa or India or another outpost of Empire, and the plots of such stories invariably tend to deal with adventurous men coping with violent situations – monsters or villainous 'savages' or 'non-white' masculinities which are more generally described in the terms: 'they' and 'us'. The characters are likely to include a beautiful heroine of unstained virtue who may be contrasted with an aggressive and vindictive 'wicked' woman, who is dangerous and whose sexual advances are to be resisted at all costs by the upright Englishman. Yet whilst the late-Victorian adventure romance was intended to be exciting, it also served an ideological function. Writers aimed to satisfy their readers' desires for escapism, showing thrills and physical danger but they also offered psychological reassurance and a familiar narrative coda, as the hero and his solid English values emerge triumphant. As Rob Dixon points out in *Writing the Colonial Adventure*, supporters of these swashbuckling romances also saw them 'as serving to deflect attention away from the dangerous unpleasantness of realism and decadence, which fostered introspection, unmanliness and morbidity.'[4] In an essay 'About Fiction' (1887) Rider Haggard condemned foreign 'Naturalistic' novelists like Emile Zola, for their interest in 'lewd', 'unmanly' subjects. By contrast, the supporters of 'King Romance', as the critic, Andrew Lang, put it, aimed to write for men and to reclaim the territory of the English novel.[5]

Stoker's own recorded comments on his 'outdoor' books, as he termed them, are few and far between. 'I dare not stop to think' is Jonathan Harker's reflection in *Dracula* as he writes furiously away, and when, in 1911, the novelist, Lucy Clifford, asked him about the genesis of *The Lair of the White Worm* ('How on earth did that strange story come into your head...?') Stoker seems to have remained silent.[6] It is tempting to see him trying to exploit a sub-genre, which he knew was popular, in another bid for literary success. Nonetheless, it was clearly a genre in which he felt comfortable and confident and which resulted in a good many critical plaudits. Thus, in 1895 *The St James's Gazette* made the following comments on his Scottish tale of smuggling and forbidden love *The Watter's Mou*:

> The 'Acme' Library which has nothing to do with snakes, by the way, having started auspiciously with Mr Conan Doyle's 'Parasite' will add to its reputation for combining literary art and publishers craft by its second volume, Mr Bram Stoker's "Watter's Mou" – a bracing little story of strong emotion and heroic action. It is a tale of the rugged Aberdeenshire coast...For an equally vivid realisation of such a theatre of action that is presented in the "Watter's Mou" one must go back to "Guy Mannering"....a fascinating romance...admirably imagined and told with a lucid simplicity that transports the reader at once to the scene of action and makes him an interested spectator upon the spot of the sorrowful drama which is enacted.[7]

Working within the confines of the 'theatre of action' and its display of 'heroic action', Stoker went on to become, as the critic W. F. Purvis noted in 1911, 'prodigious', mixing different genres, different settings and themes, working with the supernatural, the Gothic, the utopian, and the topical, indulging his taste for landscapes full of wild scenery and monstrous life-forms, showing examples of ostentatiously heroic behaviour, whilst painting nightmarish scenarios where the primal self threatens to overwhelm the civilized.[8] In this chapter, we will focus on three texts: the Irish novel, *The Snake's Pass* (1890), the Ruritanian romance, *The Lady of the Shroud* (1909), and the horror novel, *The Lair of the White Worm* (1911).

For the most part, critics have tended to ignore these novels, viewing them as second-rate, or – as far as *The Lair of the White Worm* is concerned – rather embarrassing. If these texts have any interest at all, the argument goes, it is as quaint examples of hack work produced for the mass market by a man who was careless about what he wrote or, in the case of *The Lair of the White Worm*, was in the advanced stages of syphilitic-induced dementia. As novels they clearly *are* written with an eye to what Stoker thought would sell but I will be arguing that they are also interesting in their own right: they demonstrate Stoker's mastery of different narrative techniques; they demonstrate his concern with morality, offer scope for reader-identification; they feed anxieties prompted by 'real-life' events but they are also didactic and offer reassurance. They demonstrate too, how Stoker writes within – and out of – the ideological values of his age. What is also particularly striking about the stories is that they are all played out in very specifically described locations, an obvious testament to Stoker's interests in the interplay between character and environment and in the clash of cultures. As Stoker readers, we ourselves quickly become accustomed to an emphasis on setting, the merging of actual and metaphorical landscapes and the complexity with which seemingly magical/supernatural elements mingle with more obviously realist or 'factual' elements. *The Snake's Pass* takes Ireland for its setting, and also as part of its subject; the action of *The Lady of the Shroud* begins in England and its central protagonist is English but quickly shifts to the Land of the Blue Mountains (a mythical Balkan state); the final novel, *The Lair of the White Worm* reverses the hero's journey away from England and is concerned with the arrival of a young Australian in rural Derbyshire, a landscape saturated with evidence of its ancient Celtic past and in which he is plunged into a nightmare of death and destruction. The 'queer atmosphere', as Lucy Clifford described it, of this novel is dependent, like *Dracula,* on the gap between what seems to be and what is: the fact that the beautiful sophisticate, Lady Arabella March is also a rapacious antediluvian monster with murderous designs forces the reader to recognize the close connections between the human world and that of the primal beast.

In this chapter, I want also to contextualize these novels by considering them in the light of some of the areas of contemporary debate current at the time in which Stoker was writing. First there is the nationalist/imperialist dimension. Stoker invariably used his stories as vehicles for considering topical questions about nationalism, race and empire which, by the 1890s and early 1900s, were being publicly debated in the face of political transformations – in particular the challenges to Britain's imperial dominance posed by Germany and the United States, the humiliations of the Boer War, and the rise of the New Imperialism, with its calls for a new civilizing mission in the colonies. Stoker's own addiction to the glamour of the imperial project is made clear in his *Personal Reminiscences*, in which he points out that the English have a 'glorious' mission to fulfil among the 'inferior' races' and waxes lyrical about 'the unity and glory of Empire...in all its bewildering, myriad beauty' as it manifested itself during the Coronation Gala organized by the Lyceum for Edward VII in 1903. (*PR* I 366; 342)

The second context that I will consider is that of masculinity. Throughout his adult life Stoker cultivated an image of a robust 'manly' man, famously addicted to weightlifting, running and swimming, and, whilst they are not necessarily self-portraits, he often takes such men as the basis for his novels. As I noted in the previous chapter, what Stoker's novels tend to have in common is their deep engagement with the questions of how uncertainty and change in the modern world affect the role of men, questions which are informed by political transformations, and what recent critics have recognized as a wider sense of a 'crisis' in masculinity emerging during the *fin de siècle*, a widespread 'male malaise'.[9] The waning of Victorianism, the impetus which the 'Woman Question' seemed to be gathering, after the passing of the Married Women's Property Act (1882) and the Matrimonial Causes Acts of (1882; 1893), the sudden 'plague', as it seemed to many, of New Women, homosexuals and 'inverts' like Oscar Wilde, the continuing impact of urbanization and the recruiting campaigns for the Boer War which revealed that 60 per cent of men were physically unfit for military service – all meant that it was easy to regard hard-won standards of masculinity, like many other aspects of Victorian culture, as being in a state of transition and decay. In Andrew Wynter's popular and often reprinted medical treatise *The Borderland of Insanity* (first published in 1877) modern men were described as being in 'Mazeland' and 'Driftland', without a 'controlling power'. Wynter explained that without the enforced discipline of military service, the mind and bodies of young middle and upper-class men would 'first stiffen from disuse and then rot from the decay of a vitality which it never properly brought into play.'[10] One solution seemed to be to toughen up young men by sending them on colonial service. This was also the message of a much-reported speech 'Frontiers', given at Oxford in 1907 by Lord Curzon, a former Viceroy of India. Curzon was in no doubt about the benefits of 'Frontier expansion for the Anglo-Saxon national character'. 'I am one of those who hold that in this larger atmosphere, on the outskirts of Empire, where the machine is relatively impotent and the individual is strong, is to be found an ennobling and invigorating stimulus for our youth, saving them alike from the corroding ease and the morbid excitements of Western civilisation.'[11] In the adventure romance of the 1890s, the codes and ideals that governed Anglo-Saxon gentlemanly behaviour played a large part in the way in which characters were represented, helping to bolster up the consoling and extremely potent myth that 'the English were still the superior imperial power and that Englishmen presented an example of moral uprightness and physical excellence....'[12] That this is also one of the most striking features of fictions produced a decade later, in the years leading up to World War I, is a point made by Sandra Kemp, Charlotte Mitchell and David Trotter in their *Companion to Edwardian Fiction*. As they explain: 'Edwardian writers devised a new kind of hero: one who would adequately represent a nation which though sunk in decadence was still sound at heart, and likely to respond to the scent of battle', and whose story was in effect a kind of rite of passage with an identity discovered in daring deeds and restoring order.[13]

THE SNAKE'S PASS

Many of these obsessions are very powerfully played out in Stoker's first full-length novel, *The Snake's Pass*. First published as a weekly serial in the conservative Sunday newspaper *The People* (20 July – 30 November 1890), *The Snake's Pass* was an attempt by Stoker to bring him a new and popular audience. It is also a text in which he introduced a number of themes and modes of representation that would be repeated throughout his writing. The outline of the story is relatively straightforward. Arthur Severn, a young Englishman, visits Connemara in the west of Ireland; the country is still at this time, one of England's colonies. Here, Arthur is not only captivated by the beauty of the landscape but realizes that he feels alive for the first time: 'exalted in a strange way and impressed at the same time with a new sense of the reality of things. It almost seemed as if through

75

that opening valley, with the mighty Atlantic beyond and the piling up of the storm clouds overhead, I passed into a new and more real life' (*SP* 4). There is a fairy-tale dimension to the opening pages of the novel, with echoes of 'Sleeping Beauty'. However it soon transpires that, as he 'looks with new eyes on the beauty and reality of the world', Arthur is also being educated into the ways of 1880s Ireland. Arthur discovers that this is a still-feudal agricultural society, one that is struggling for survival in the face of (legal) persecution at the hands of Murtagh 'Black' Murdock, a melodramatically sinister 'gombeen man' or moneylender who extracts money out of the debt-ridden local farmers until they are forced to relinquish their property to him. When Arthur falls in love with the virtuous Norah Joyce, the daughter of Murdock's chief victim, he chivalrously attempts to assist her and her father. In this he is aided by an old school-friend, Dick Sutherland, a geologist who is now working for Murdock, mapping disputed land on the hill of Knockcalltecrore, land which contains a sinister 'shifting bog' and is rumoured to be the site of golden treasure. One result of Murdock's excavation is to disturb the natural landscape and, in a violent storm, the bog collapses. Arthur is saved by Norah but Murdock is sucked in to his death. Murdock's removal and the disappearance of the bog is the means by which harmony is restored. Arthur marries Norah, thus establishing a new Anglo-Irish family, and ensuring that under his protection, she and the rest of the local Irish population become part of a recognizably English model of community with Arthur as benevolent land-owner. Overall this story demonstrates, Arthur tells the reader, 'all the happiness men and women may win for themselves' (*SP* 250).

How then does the *The Snake's Pass* fit the pattern of the adventure romance? First, there is its narrator, Arthur. He is indisputably the novel's central concern – the hero of his own story – and is a fairly recognizable type. Arthur's most obvious literary ancestor is David Balfour in R. L. Stevenson's *Kidnapped* and *Catriona*. He also carries traces of some of the more naïve heroes of Walter Scott, for example Edward Waverley in *Waverley* (1814) and (going further back), Daniel Defoe's *Robinson Crusoe* (1719). Arthur first appears to the reader as a deeply-divided personality, orphaned as a child, wealthy but a young man whose early life has left him alone, innocent and emotionally deprived, and consumed by an overwhelming sense that he is an 'outsider' until the opportunity to travel brings him the opportunity to experience – if not a complete re-birthing – at least an attempt at 'overcoming the negative forces that had hitherto dominated my life.'

A second way in which *The Snake's Pass* fits the template of the adventure romance is in its interest in the interplay between character and environment. As I have suggested, this is a feature of Stoker's work more generally. Repeatedly, he chooses to set his fiction around a clash between one of his protagonists (usually a young man) and a remote, unfamiliar location, an encounter that is both physical and psychological. What he offers his readers is not just the unknown but a new experience or new way of looking at something that may have been known. As we have seen, both *The Primrose Path* and *Dracula* have such encounters as a starting point: Jerry O'Sullivan's sense of dislocation in metropolitan London and Jonathan Harker's mental breakdown in Transylvania. The stories of William Barrow in *The Watter's Mou* (1895) and Harold An Wolf in *The Man* (1905) also involve this device of the young man plunged into confusion and the accompanying sense of personal fear and paranoia this provokes. *The Snake's Pass* is essentially structured on the disjunction between the surface Ireland – the Emerald Isle of popular mythology – and the dark underside, which threatens to plunge its English hero, Arthur Severn, into chaos. His first encounter with Norah Joyce becomes a sensuous and symbolic moment on the windswept mountain of Knocknacar where their love blossoms in idyllic communion with natural surroundings: 'High above us towered the everlasting rocks; the green of natures planting lay beneath our feet...the sound of the sea and the beating of our hearts were hymns of praise to nature and to nature's God' (*SP* 132). However, there are also sinister, unnamed presences lurking in the countryside that Arthur becomes aware of but cannot see.

> After a while there came more light into the sky, or my eyes became accustomed to the darkness, for I thought that now and again I beheld 'men as trees walking'. Presently something dark and massive seemed outlined in the sky before us – a blackness projected onto a darkness.We plodded on for a while, and the hill before us

seemed to overshadow whatever glimmer of light there was, for the darkness grew more profound than ever. (*SP* 44)

These uncanny and Gothic elements of the landscape are encapsulated in the figure of the notorious 'shifting bog'. Again and again Arthur comes back to it as a central reference point, a symbolic representation of the monstrous and the 'unfathomable':

> The wind had now dropped away; the morning light struck full over the hill, and we could see clearly. The sound of the waves dashing on the rocks below, and the booming of the distant breakers filled the air – but through it came another sound, the like of which I had never heard, and the like of which I hope, in God's providence, I shall never hear again – a long low gurgle, with something of a sucking sound; something terrible – resistless – and with a sort of hiss in it, as of seething waters striving to be free.
>
> Then the convulsion of the bog grew greater; it almost seemed as if some monstrous living thing was deep under the surface and waiting to escape....And then came a mighty roar and a gathering rush. The side of the hill below us seemed to burst. Murdock threw up his arms – we heard his wild cry as the roof of the house and he with it was in an instant sucked below the surface of the heaving mass. (*SP* 229-30)

The Irish landscape features almost as a character in *The Snake's Pass*, a powerful influence on its English hero. It is as much a psychological place as it is a physical one. As the landscape's chief feature (even the novel's chief character), the treacherous bog, 'a carpet of death', swollen with incessant rainfall, seems to have taken on the attributes of the legendary serpent-monster, threatening the lives of all who approach. For the novel's hero, the 'mighty mass' of the 'Vast bog' also helps compound his own identity crisis. As an orphan whose own parents drowned as they crossed the Channel, the presumed horrors of the watery bog prompt Arthur to internalize it, adding to his sense of isolation and fears of personal oblivion, and in a dream he imagines it wiping out all traces of himself: 'We clung together in terror....And then over the cliff poured the whole mass of the bog, foul-smelling, foetid, terrible, and of endless night....' (*SP* 206). The fear of burial or immersion in the monstrous slime and the accompanying annihilation of 'self' is recognizably Oedipal, it is also a part of the middle-class Gothic 'stock in trade'; the monster which needs to be tamed in order that imperial civilization can be maintained. It represents too the 'constant sense that the divide between the stable and unstable is itself unstable, that the line can not be held.'[14]

The bog is also the novel's central (and very topical) metaphor for Anglo-Irish political and historical relations. This becomes clearer when we remember that *The Snake's Pass* did not spring into being out of an historical or social vacuum. There has been considerable interest recently in the ways in which *The Snake's Pass* – a novel written by an Irishman set in Ireland but with English heroes among alien people – can be seen to intersect with late-Victorian debates about the Irish Question, the Land War of 1879–82, and the Home Rule Crisis of the 1880s and 1890s. Arthur describes how he is warned 'against going out too much alone at night' for fear that he should run into 'the moonlighters who now and again raided the district', members of the Irish National Land League who killed their opponents under cover of darkness.[15] It is worth noting that during the months of the novel's serialization in *The People,* the same paper was simultaneously printing reports that resonate with Stoker's text. These included worried commentaries about the radical nationalist MP Charles Stuart Parnell, his attacks on William Gladstone and rioting in Irish towns. Part of Stoker's pride in his first full-length novel stemmed from his integration of Irish rural and British imperial ideologies and his construction of the novel as an idealized alternative to, and fictional substitute for, other bloody operations of British government. One reason for writing *The Snake's Pass* seems to have been for Stoker to educate his British audience about the Irish people, a people whose independent existence was seen by the British as politically and economically undesirable. Ireland was a poor, under-invested colony, regarded by its absentee English landlords as an abundance of land and a ready supply of cheap labour. Stoker offered the novel to the Prime Minister William Gladstone as a commentary on the 'centuries-old Irish troubles', later boasting that 'as Mr Gladstone was then full of Irish matters, my book being of Ireland and dealing with Irish ways and especially of a case of oppression by a "gombeen" man under a loan secured on land, interested him....' (*PR* I 29)

Looked at in this light, it is perhaps not surprising that it is the bog that comes to dominate the whole novel. As Nicholas Daly has suggested, there is a sense that Stoker regards the bog as a metaphor for the 'nightmare of history', the unruliness and untameable nature of Ireland and the long violent history of Irish hostility to English rule. In *Modernism, Romance and the Fin de Siècle*, Daly argues that the bog is a symbol of the Celtic past and also stands 'for those aspects of the country which have been most resistant to the colonial project, the bog is that which, while yielding fails to keep the imprint made by the work of colonization – the spade sinks in but it leaves no trace when it is withdrawn'.[16] In another recent article 'Some Hysterical Hatred: History, Hysteria and the Literary Revival', Luke Gibbons has taken this analysis one step further by suggesting that the bog (which is almost alive) can be read like one of Sigmund Freud's hysterical subjects; the colonial violence it embodies is metaphoric of a repressed (Irish) psychic structure. It is for this reason that the bog needs to be tamed. It represents 'a dangerous bolting hole for the wild Irish who will not come within the pale of civilization'.[17] It is only through Murdock's being sucked into the mud, merging literally with the ground that the conflict is resolved and by which Arthur, Norah and the rest of the local Irish population can move forwards to the prospect of a new brighter future and establish a new more harmonious community.[18]

In terms of Stoker's output as a whole, *The Snake's Pass* is a significant work. It is the last of what we might call Stoker's 'apprenticeship' works, in its setting still close to *The Primrose Path*, but possessing also the status of a bridging novel, looking forward to for instance, *The Watter's Mou, Dracula, The Mystery of the Sea, The Lady of the Shroud* and *The Lair of the White Worm*, especially in its emphasis on 'psychic unease' and the way in which it makes use of the 'locus suspectus' to use Freud's phrase (literally 'the suspect place').[19] We also see how, in keeping with its quest-narrative origins, the conflict between Arthur and Murdock is sometimes given almost mythic status, with Arthur's role being to restore fertility and life back to the district, whilst his vividly imagined adversary Murdock (a reincarnation, it is hinted, of the evil King of the Snakes), sucks its lifeblood. This fantastical dimension to the novel is encouraged by the way in which Murdock, an archetypal villain has his persecution of his neighbours repeatedly ascribed a 'wolfish' or 'devilish' aspect. Murdock certainly raises thr suspicion in the other characters of the novel that he is not quite human. He appears for the first time, listening at the window of Widow Kelligan's inn as a storm rages. Like Count Dracula in the later novel, he is devoured by the shadows as he leaves and the people inside hear only the 'clattering of his horses feet on the rock road' as the wind howls round. Murdock reappears later as a 'human shaped wolf, a "wild beast, a "savage"' (*SP* 87; 36). He is the 'monster' who must be quelled so that order can be restored.

What is also especially interesting about *The Snake's Pass* is the way it holds in place Stoker's interest in his characters as social and sexual middle-class subjects forced to deal with the 'Other', albeit with evident distaste. Considerable space is also given over to the modelling of gentlemanly conduct. For instance, we are encouraged to contemplate in Dick Sutherland an example of the modern, properly English man. Dick, who lacks any marked individuality, is a familiar type in nineteenth century adventure romances; a model of manhood produced by Stoker's, and indeed the genre's, fixation with the construction of gendered identities, and by the cult of the 'manly' boy and the 'man's man'. A professional man and engineer, his personality is built up by his association with some of the qualities considered typically masculine in Stoker's day: logic, rational thinking, science. In terms of the hero's own development, Arthur Severn's providential reunion with this old school friend sets in motion the course of action by which he searches for, measures and establishes his own masculine identity. Arthur 'thank(s) God for loyal and royal manhood' (*SP* 136), represses his own (sexual) attraction to Dick's 'handsome' masculinity, and expels the (un-manly) villain from the community. What is crucial for Stoker here is the need to make a distinction between the upright young Englishmen and the dastardly Black Murdock. Much of this is staged in class terms. Black Murdock is not part of Arthur and Dick's 'set' and he is presented as the antithesis of healthy manhood. In one scene he is called 'a dastardly soul' by Arthur and warned 'take care how you cross her path or mine again, or you shall rue it to the last day of your life. Come. Come Norah, it is not fit that you should contaminate your eyes or your ears with the presence of this wretch!' The offence to Arthur's delicate sensibilities caused by the presence of Black Murdock is a reminder that he represents the inversion of the gentlemanly masculine ideal, who to the Englishmen is also 'other'. Dick's contemptuous announcement to Black Murdock that 'a fellow of your stamp...[can hardly] understand a gentleman's feelings...' echoes this (*SP* 60). Yet quite how the reader is meant to respond to this is not clear. There is certainly some evidence that these denunciations were regarded as laughably melodramatic by some of Stoker's contemporaries. In 1890 a reviewer for the *Athenaeum* commented that Stoker's attempt to make 'the two heroes...almost equally high-minded, scrupulous and self sacrificing' meant that 'they carry these virtues to a pitch which amounts to absurdity'.[20] Murdock's rapacious (sexual) designs on Norah, his wish to defile not only her father's land but his daughter as well, do suggest that his origins lie not in the supernatural but in melodrama and certainly his behaviour provokes appropriately heightened language from Stoker's heroes. At the same time, these exchanges signal that our perception of Murdock is in some degree a product of Arthur's conventional, even naïve, perceptual framework through which Murdock (a man of 'low character' (*SP* 61) who has clearly not received the benefits of a public school education) is focused. We see the position that Arthur, as the seemingly reliable narrator of the story, is writing from. It involves an unquestioned assumption of British superiority over all foreigners. He expresses not only an emotional feeling but also a social and ideological attitude, one that provides much of the momentum of the narrative.

Like many imperial romances of the 1890s, one of the narrative goals of *The Snake's Pass* is to (re)establish the rightful ownership of a particular stretch of territory and establish the moral rights of those who control it. However there is also some confusion about the ending of *The Snake's Pass*, which results from the fact that the narrative follows two slightly different trajectories. One reading of the story is that Stoker merely reprises a version of the adventure or imperial romance plot, where the hero (a product of good breeding and a public school education) manages to overcome the physical dangers he encounters and is rewarded with lifelong devotion from grateful 'natives.' As Stoker's contemporary reviewers recognized, his story does fit this mould. It starts by charting the arrival of an Englishman in an outpost of Empire, a society where colonized and colonizers are unable to cohere; it finishes by demonstrating the possibility of social order and by extension, universal well-being: 'life not as it is but as it ought to be' as a reviewer for the *Academy* noted.[21] This new utopia is created by the mediating presence of the gentleman hero, Arthur, who, whilst he is aware of the romantic, emotional aspect of his own temperament, going so far as to marry (rather than merely seduce) a native woman, does not lose himself completely or turn his back on the county of his birth: once an Englishman always an Englishman. Whilst Stoker is careful not to say that it is because its occupants are a 'lesser breed' (as Rudyard Kipling termed it) that causes the problems in this outpost of Empire, he *does* suggest that these colonial subjects need to be 'helped' to move forward by a healthy middle-class young man. Thus Arthur marries Norah, buys her father's land at a knock-down price and discovers a valuable reserve of limestone. This discovery enables him to renovate the district (using the latest scientific expertise) and put its picturesque body of natives to gainful employment in the limestone quarry whilst setting up 'a plan for building houses for them – good solid stone houses, with proper offices and farmyards.' The fact that the local colonial population happily accepts this new state of affairs is a gesture of affirmation, on their part, of their role as subjects. However, a more cynical reader might also say that Arthur Severn's own arrival in Ireland is, like the bog, merely another kind of irruption, and his narrative is written so as to justify a piece of aggressive English history-making. Arthur is an explorer but also an exploiter, whose instinct is to take possession – both of the girl and the land.

THE LADY OF THE SHROUD

The generic formula of the adventure romance – lots of male bonding and English snobbery – in which the Englishman is forced to bring the so-called 'subject races' into line – recurs in different variations throughout Stoker's work. *The Mystery of the Sea* (1902) has an American treasure-seeking heroine Marjorie

Drake team up with the aptly-named Archibald Hunter to put down the 'swarthy' Cubans and a 'beast' of 'a buck nigger from Noo Orleans' as he is described.[22] In *The Man* (discussed in more detail in chapter 4) the 'Viking'-like Harold An Wolf discovers his true sense of selfhood and the discovery of his place in Britain's imperial structure not by lying about languidly at home like his degenerate-effeminate counterpart Leonard Everard, but by taking a false name – the Crusoe-esque 'John Robinson' – and by travelling to Alaska. Here he enacts the role of a pioneer in a new land, submitting himself in a conventional manly manner to 'The Lesson of the Wilderness'. It is through his living a life of 'danger and strenuous toil' that he is regenerated and comes to take on the qualities of 'self-reliant manhood'.

We observe something similar in Stoker's novel of 1909, *The Lady of the Shroud*. What is at issue here, however, is not the scramble for America but Europe. Specifically the focus is on the Balkan peninsula (the so-called 'back-door of Europe'), a region populated by supposedly primitive peoples and despotic warlords, and one which, as Vesna Goldsworthy points out, 'a particularly British orientalising rhetoric' identified in the 1900s 'as a corrupt and undisciplined Other.'[23] Into the mysterious 'Land of the Blue Mountains' strides, or rather flies, Rupert Sent Ledger, an orphaned 'pauper' relative of a snobbish aristocratic family and as much shunned by them as Arthur Severn is by his family in *The Snake's Pass*. A strong, brave, tall (6 feet 7 inches) and well-travelled man, Sent Ledger is another reliable pair of imperial hands, a 'symbol of stability' in a period of change, who can be trusted to take charge of this story of a quasi-colonial enterprise[24]. Although Sent Ledger – a kind of Edwardian 'Renaissance man' – is cultivated and well-travelled, he still holds many of the blinkered opinions of upper-class British Edwardian society. His roles as a maverick and explorer may encourage him to be more socially enlightened, but he is still an embodiment of, and adherent to, many of the attitudes of the class that has shunned him and its governing codes.

The story that follows is a relatively simple one: Rupert Sent Ledger inherits from his uncle a castle and lands in Vissarion, part of the Land of the Blue Mountains, a volatile Balkan state which is threatened by its immediate neighbours, Albania, Dalmatia, Servia and Bulgaria. As a condition of his inheritance,

Rupert is charged with supporting the local ruler, the Voivode Vissarion in the latter's attempts to impose stability and freedom. He travels to his new estate where he begins a programme of modernization, which includes importing a private army of loyal Scottish soldiers. At night he is visited by the ghostly Lady of the Shroud. The Lady is eventually revealed to be the Voivodin Teuta (daughter of the Voivode Vissarion). The false reports of her death are part of a plan to prevent her being kidnapped by Turkish agents. Rupert secretly marries Teuta but cannot prevent the kidnap. He has to rescue her from 'the worst fate of all – the harem...that dreadful life of shameful slavery.' Teuta's father is also kidnapped but Rupert flies an aeroplane to rescue him from the prison. Rupert becomes the ruler of the principality. He establishes a successful radium-mining industry and trains army units both for service at sea and the 'airship service' (LS 240). He also manages to solve the Balkan question by establishing a federation of Balkan countries under the name 'Balka.' The novel closes with a vision of utopia, as Rupert is crowned king with the crown of Balka, followed by a vast aeroplane show. Stoker announces prophetically that 'henceforth no nation with an eye for either defence or attack can hope for success without the mastery of the air'. (LS 258)

Like many of Stoker's novels, there is more to *The Lady of the Shroud* than first appears and it is interesting in a number of respects. To begin with, the novel can be situated in several contexts. It was extensively reviewed at the time of publication in 1909 and, as many reviewers noted, the novel is like many other Edwardian romances written in the years leading up to the First World War, a kind of rallying cry to Englishmen in the face of a growing Anglo-German rivalry and widespread European instability, one predicated on the assumption that what is needed is a 'national regeneration' set in motion by the efforts of right-thinking, heterosexual men.[25] The novel's contemporary resonance was remarked upon by several of its reviewers. *The Bookman*, evidently admiring Stoker's patriotism, described it as:

> a huge prophetic melodrama of the near East: he [Stoker] creates in outline at least that Balkan Federation, which may or may not be feasible, but certainly seems essential to the curbing of Austrian ambitions on the one hand and Turkish pretensions on the other.

And that is not all. He gives us a great Ruritanian Romance in the manner of Anthony Hope, or rather perhaps we should say in the fashion of Stanley Weyman, palpitating with passion, full of high colour, breathless in movement.

This last remark is significant, for as well as being carried along by what they regarded as its stirring (masculine) energy, reviewers also sought to understand the novel by locating it in terms of its genre. *The Lady of the Shroud* is a literary relative of Hope's immensely popular *The Prisoner of Zenda* (1894), as well as Weyman's best-selling spy-story *Under the Red Robe* (1894). It also has a good deal in common with another Balkan 'hit' of 1909: Dorothea Gerard's *The Red Hot Crown,* a novel inspired by the 'real-life' assassination of the King and Queen of Serbia in 1903. In all of these texts, the solution for the regeneration of enervated Edwardian men was to stride forth into the raw, untamed places of the world on a civilizing mission.

Stoker's very obvious need for money in the years following Irving's death makes it tempting to think that the main reason he wrote this novel was to cash in on another literary vogue. However, one of Stoker's aims in *The Lady of the Shroud* is a very topical one for 1909: encouraging readers to think about the ways in which the British upper-classes might be more usefully employed in the service of Empire. The need for a change in attitude is embodied in the figure of Rupert Sent Ledger's prissy, status-conscious cousin, Ernest Melton, whose self-absorption, putting self and wealth before service to the nation, is indicative of a more widespread superannuation of the aristocracy; immured in their country estates and choosing to ignore or be bypassed by twentieth-century incentives. In *The Lady of the Shroud*, Stoker, like Lord Curzon whose comments I cited earlier, suggests that it is only by cultural and geographical removal to a challenging place, far away from the over-civilized and effete conditions of modern English life, that the real salvation of young Englishmen can take place. The encounter with 'other' cultures – raw, savage, untamed – is the key to cultural and political identity and it is the non-English, uncivilized representatives of these other cultures that define or circumscribe Englishness. Initially, Rupert Sent Ledger, despite being a conspicuously 'manly' man, seems as unpromising as his cousin Ernest. He has no fixed profession and is a 'pauper' until he comes into vast wealth. It takes a voice from beyond the grave, that of his uncle (and a representative of the family's past), to push Rupert Sent Ledger into an awareness of his responsibilities to class, duty and nation, and of the ways in which 'a man of courage and ability may carve out for himself a name and place in history' (*LS* 31). It takes the experience of another displaced aristocrat, Teuta, daughter of the Balkan warlord, to remind him of the alternative – 'a life in death existence...' (*LS* 93).

Like *Dracula*, the story that follows is told through a series of supposedly 'real' documents (journals, letters, newspaper reports, travel narratives). The text also returns to some of the same ground mapped out in *Dracula*, taking in not only the occult and supernatural but also the clashes between past and present and between cultures. We have already seen the importance of the landscape in Stoker's texts – from Norah Joyce's cottage in *The Snake's Pass* and 'the wild mountain-top' at Knockcalltecrore that leaves Arthur Severn full of the sense of 'divine love', to the impregnability of Dracula's castle, which instils in Jonathan Harker the realization that 'the old centuries had, and have, powers of their own which mere modernity cannot kill' (*D* 67). *The Lady of the Shroud* continues these notions. It is most fully realized in Rupert Sent Ledger's growing attachment to the atmosphere at Vissarion, propelling him, as he puts it, into 'high-grade sentiments of poetic fancy': 'from the Castle, a huge pile of buildings of every style of architecture, from the Twelfth Century to where things seemed to stop in this dear old-world land' to his 'greediness' for 'the first ray of light over the mountains' (*LS* 55–57). The novel is also written in the same pantheistic spirit with which Stoker began in *The Snake's Pass*; like Arthur Severn, Rupert Sent Ledger is the reader's guide through a particular wild, alien landscape: 'the forests running up their silvered slopes flame-like in form, deviated here and there by great crags and outcropping rock sinews of the vast mountains' (*LS* 68). The language is poetic, by which I mean that it is more allusive than we expect to find in either fiction or indeed the Balkans in 'real-life'. As Stoker describes it, the landscape, 'a mass of Gothic cliffs, crags and ravines' also suggests the poles of experience through which Rupert must steer his course to maturity.[26] And as Rupert stands alone, looking out at the view of the mountains from his castle battlements, he muses on 'the beauty that Nature creates by the hand of her servant, Time' (*LS* 57). The reader is invited to compare the ageless hills with the transience of human life; the hills become a reminder of man's mortality but they are also life-inspiring.

Rupert Sent Ledger becomes intertwined – literally as well as figuratively – with the history of the Land of the Blue Mountains through his meeting with the eponymous Lady of the Shroud. The novel covers other familiar territory here. As we have seen, Stoker often chose to construct his stories around an enigmatic woman in possession of some dark secret. In *The Lady of the Shroud* these women include Rupert's dead mother and his unmarried aunt, Janet McKelpie (whose robust bluff Scottish common-sense only just manages to disguise the strength of her incestuous feelings for her nephew). The chief of these women, however, is the Voivodin Teuta Vissarion, the mysterious 'Lady', who is first encountered in a report in the *Journal of Occultism*: a deathly woman standing in a coffin drifting (Dracula-fashion) in an open boat along the coast. When she next appears it is to interrupt the 'pyjama-clad' Rupert Sent Ledger's sleepless thoughts on the balcony outside his bedroom: 'a woman, wrapped in white grave clothes, saturated with water, which dripped on the marble floor, making a pool which trickled slowly down the wet steps' (*LS* 69). This is followed by her appearance in Janet McKelpie's dreams as 'the shadow of Death, with 'worms crawl[ing] round the flagstone at her feet' (*LS* 88).

As it turns out, the Lady of the Shroud is not the monstrous *femme fatale* she first appears and the complicated schema of her relations with the other characters are used more as a means of critiquing the ways in which racial and sexual identities are created, deployed and understood. The cataleptic state of the scantily-clad woman, her solitary wanderings at night and her return at daybreak to the bowels of the church of St Sava all present a form of 'narrative teasing' as Victor Sage has noted.[27] 'What was that?' asks Rupert Sent Ledger, and his brain is thrown into 'a whirl' as he tries to make sense of this apparition. Is she a 'lady'? Is she 'all woman – living woman'? (*LS* 69; 74; 110) Is she a victim? A 'fallen' woman? A foreigner? Another 'bloofer lady' (like Lucy Westenra in *Dracula*)? Or is she 'dead' or 'Un-dead – a Vampire with one foot in Hell and one on Earth'

(*LS* 110)? All of these 'doubts and imaginings' run through Sent Ledger's mind as he 'strained her dear body to [his]...as her lovely eyes seemed to devour him (*LS* 78; 112). He cannot decide:

> I was interrupted, cut short...not by any words but by the frightened look in her eyes and the fear-mastered way in which she shrank away from me. I suppose in reality she could not be paler than she looked when the colour-absorbing moonlight fell on her; but on the instant all semblance of living seemed to shrink and fall away, and she looked in dread as if in some awful way held in thrall. But for the movement of the pitiful glances she would have seemed of soulless marble, so deadly cold did she look....No! I could not accept belief as to her being other than a living woman of souls and sense, of flesh and blood, of all the sweet and passionate instincts of true and perfect womanhood. (*LS* 112; 127)

Like Stoker's other male characters in similar situations, Rupert's meetings with this odd woman throw him into a 'harassing state of uncertainty' about his own 'consciousness and identity', 'so vast as to overwhelm me....I suppose it must be what men suffered...under enchantments in old times. I am but as a straw whirled in the resistless eddies of a whirlpool...' (*LS* 78; 105–106). 'I was not myself' he announces (*LS* 104). One of the reasons why the Lady upsets Rupert's sense of who he himself is is that her appearance confuses his ideas about women and 'ladies' upon which his own English masculine identity is founded. William Hughes notes that the behaviour of the Lady of the Shroud, including her scorn for his prudish objections to the paucity of her clothing, is 'beyond his [Rupert's] western, bourgeois experience'.[28] Like Arthur Severn with Norah Joyce in *The Snake's Pass*, Rupert tries to respond as a 'true gentleman' (*LS* 105) to those elements of the strange woman's appearance and behaviour which he recognizes as matching his idea of respectable, middle-class womanhood: sweetness, 'girlish inno-cence', helplessness, circumspection, weakness. Yet despite having 'pledged' himself to help her, there is still an 'awful moment' when he is struck by the fear that he has let loose on other men one of those rampant female vampires 'who live on the blood of the living, and bring eternal damnation as well as death with the poison of their dreadful kisses' (*LS* 113).

In a recent essay, 'Crowning the King, Mourning his Mother',

Lisa Hopkins, in one of the few feminist treatments of the novel, points to its overriding concern with motherhood and suggests that the reason why it takes so long for Stoker's lonely, isolated hero to realize the Lady's real (living) identity is because of 'his own psychological need to equate her with his loved dead mother.' According to Hopkins: 'In this novel you need see a vampire only if you wish to – Rupert does so wish. For him, it is indeed only a dead woman who can make the place "homey", and by re-imagining the Dracula figure as both female and as welcomed – a "homey" visitant – Stoker offers a graphic vision of the...pre-Oedipal mother'.[29] Succumbing to the Lady's maternal embrace is comforting but it also delays his psychological development.

Rupert may mourn his mother but it is only by uncovering the Lady of the Shroud's real identity as Teuta, the rightful heiress of the Land of the Blue Mountain, that Rupert's own identity crisis is resolved. The main preoccupation of the second half of the book is the restoration of Teuta's father, the Voivode, to his rightful throne and it gives the hero a real purpose in life. This is Rupert's real adventure and intriguingly the fight for the crown results in a restoration of Rupert also. He regenerates himself as a combination of 'Viking' warrior and chivalrous knight, a worthy descendent of his ancestors:

> I only wished to do the woman good – to serve her in some way – to secure her some benefit by any means, no matter how difficult, which might be in my power...whether she was an ordinary woman (or an extraordinary woman, for the matter of that) in some sore and terrible straits; or else one who lay under some dreadful condition, only partially alive, and not mistress of herself or her acts. Whatever her condition might be, there was in my own feeling a superfluity of affection for her....As she rested, half sitting and half lying on the pile of cushions she was...the veritable perfect woman of the dreams of a man, be he young or old. To have such a woman sit by his hearth...might well be a rapture to any man. (LS 94–5; 103)

The attraction between Rupert and the Lady however is considerably more than just physical or emotional. Exiled from her royalist origins, Teuta, like her father, is desperate to return to the estate culture that she understands as her natural place. She is drawn to the society that is hers by right of birth. The passionate liaison with Rupert shows this natural realignment operating at its most intimate levels. Anxious to ensure the survival of the race, Teuta is drawn to Rupert in bio-sociological or eugenicist terms as a potential stud. Everyone in the novel sees his body as a model of male beauty: 'magnificent, towering above everybody', 'bronzed', 'big and strong'. These physical traits do not simply signify Rupert's masculinity but also that he will be a promising addition to the ancient Vissarion gene pool. He possesses a 'lion's heart meet for a great body' (*LS* 152).

Rupert's own attraction to Teuta as a 'mate' is based, as has been said, on her vulnerable beauty and her dependent femininity but once again it is hard not to notice that, like Arthur Servern in *The Snake's Pass*, the hero's reward in this romance plot is both the girl *and* the valuable land, rich with mineral deposits. Although Stoker has earlier undermined the idea of marriages based on money and status in his representation of Ernest Melton this is forgotten about at the end, with Rupert as ruler of the Land of the Blue Mountains (in his own right) and King of Balka, as the father of Teuta's son, also called Rupert, and thus the progenitor of a new royal dynasty. This rise in status is accomplished without any real disruption of the social order and the plot encourages us to believe that Rupert's rise is a natural one – as natural as his growth into a specimen of English perfection.

Another destination of Stoker's novel is a much less openly signalled confirmation of conventional gender roles. Several critics have noted the way in which, having displayed both a 'class-based imperiousness' and a 'Teutonic militancy' in her initial encounters with Rupert, Teuta is stripped of these qualities.[30] Lisa Hopkins observes of Teuta how, once her 'real' identity is revealed she 'presents herself as a figure fully submissive to patriarchal authority' serving only as a 'powerful enabling mechanism for Rupert Sent Ledger'.[31] At the end of the novel, Rupert's narrative is structured in such a way as to celebrate this closing down of the physiological and psychological gap between the Lady of the Shroud and Teuta. After her marriage Teuta's identity is much more clearly defined, at least in Rupert's eyes: 'Not a vampire, but a poor harassed creature doomed to terrible woes, but a splendid woman' (*LS* 150).

Although Rupert's diary substitutes the figure of wife for that of vampire fairly unproblematically, the reader who reads on to the end of the novel will see that there are some unanswered questions about this version of genteel femininity and about the cultural frame of reference that sustains it. It is difficult not to notice that even when she is freed from her coffin and the Turks into the 'Christian' hands of Rupert and his aunt to be exalted as 'a symbol and type of woman's devotion' (*LS* 191), Teuta still exists in a state of confinement. 'Like a good wife she obeyed' Rupert reports (*LS* 82). Feminist critics would thus say that much of the power of this novel (as in the case of *Dracula*) comes from the similarities between the heroines' subterranean existence in crypts and their burial in domestic spaces. Once married, Teuta's wearing of the symbol of subjection – her shroud – on all public occasions becomes less to do with commemorating her bravery than bowing to the inevitable, an inevitable that is executed both in the public and private spheres.[32]

The Lady of the Shroud is in many respects a text that collects together many of the different elements of Stoker's work. It testifies to the reading public's interest in the amateur hero and, although its title suggests feminine subject matter, the novel is as much about men as about women – the female protagonists being mostly occupied with pleasing the novel's hero and living happily ever after. Both Janet McKelpie and Teuta end up making do with less, but in settling for less they are, readers are told, entirely contented. In the male-orientated *The Lady of the Shroud*, Stoker thus returns to the ideological demonstration he had set down so firmly at the end of *Dracula* and would try to reinforce in his final novel, *The Lair of the White Worm* (1911), namely the necessary internalization by women of the social structures against which they might be expected to rebel, together with the recurrent spectacle of what Kathleen Blake describes as 'male dominance as a fact and a wish.'[33]

THE LAIR OF THE WHITE WORM

Like *Dracula*, *The Lair of the White Worm* has always held a special place amongst Stoker's novels, although it is only very recently that it has begun to attract the kind of critical attention bestowed on its more famous forerunner. Its 'queer' atmosphere bemused many of Stoker's contemporaries; others, like the *Times Literary*

Supplement, saw it as symptomatic of a wider cultural malaise, a part of the degenerate aesthetics that marked popular fiction and proof of how Stoker himself had 'degenerated'.[34] In her introduction to the 1996 Oxford World Classics edition of *Dracula,* Maud Ellman suggests that the novel reveals Stoker as 'prude and pornographer at once, each of these impulses apparently exacerbated by the fury of the other.'[35] For others, *The Lair of the White Worm* is now a 'classic', or at least a 'camp classic', and – like *Dracula* – a text that has been brought back to life by the (often lurid) readings it seems able to take on board. Like *Dracula* and *The Jewel of Seven Stars* it has spawned a film version – Ken Russell's cult-ish 1988 version, all black leather and bondage – roundly dismissed for its 'woefully clichéd imagery and hysterical acting style.'[36] At the same time, a sudden spurt of critical interest in *The Lair of the White Worm* has meant that it is beginning to be taken, like *Dracula* and the 1890s, as a key text of its time, responding to a range of contemporary debates – theories of race, mesmerism, degeneration, and feminism. In a recent article 'Why White?: Worms and Skin in Bram Stoker's Later Fiction', David Glover even suggests that 'Stoker's last novel can serve as a kind of *summa* for Stoker's entire *oeuvre...*'.[37]

Unlike the other novels discussed in this chapter, the setting for *The Lair of the White Worm* is England – Derbyshire – a region which bears the archaeological traces of Britain's ancient Celtic past. It is 1860. Into this wilderness comes Adam Salton, a young, energetic Australian, who has come to meet his great-uncle Richard Salton, who may select Adam as the heir to his estate, Lesser Hill, if he proves suitable. The estate in question is bordered by three other properties, Castra Regis, belonging to Edgar Caswell, the last in a long line of cruel local landlords, who has an interest in mesmerism and lusts after Lilla (one of two young women living at Mercy Farm). Adam, meanwhile, falls in love with Lilla's Burmese cousin, Mimi. They try to protect Lilla both from the predatory Caswell and from Lady Arabella March, who owns a house in 'Diana's Grove', the most ancient part of the region. The transgressive female embodied in Lucy Westenra is developed a bit more in Lady Arabella, a beautiful widow who – it turns out – is possessed by the spirit and body of a primeval serpent, making her the extreme form of the demonic, sexually-aggressive woman – she is literally a monster. Like Lucy, Arabella is dangerous because she hides – albeit unconvincingly – her malignity behind the appearance of the elegant, harmless Edwardian lady:

> She was certainly good to look at in herself, and her dress alone was sufficient to attract attention. She was clad in some soft white stuff, which clung close to her form, showing to the full every movement of her sinuous figure. She was tall and exceedingly thin. Her eyes appeared to be weak, for she wore large spectacles which seemed to be of green glass....She wore a close-fitting cap of some fine fur of dazzling white. Coiled round her white throat was a large necklace of emeralds whose profusion of colour quite outshone the green of her spectacles....Her voice was very peculiar, very low and sweet, and so soft that the dominant note was of sibilation. Her hands, too, were peculiar – long, flexible, white, with a strange movement of waving gently to and fro...The heartiness with which she spoke and warmth of her words – not of her manner which was abnormally cold and distant – repelled him, made him suspicious. (*LWW* 32–3)

This description will be familiar to readers of a good deal of Victorian and Edwardian fiction in which, as Lyn Pykett has noted, it is fairly common for femininity to be defined as 'duplicity' and to represent the idea of 'woman' in terms of 'impersonation, performance or masquerade.'[38] It also highlights the difficulties for men of recognizing (and hence controlling) women's 'Jekyll and Hyde' tendencies, their dual existence. Lady Arabella is represented as naturally unstable because she is a woman. As a woman she has a capacity for cunning, which is denounced as feminine and ultimately monstrous, and the novel taps into a male paranoia that the fashionable trappings of ladylike gentility are exactly that – trappings that cover monstrous female passion and self-interest.

At first glance, the narrative that Lady Arabella creates for herself seems to be a fairly mundane (if unpleasant) story of self-help in which she intends to exploit her beauty and respectable social standing. Her estate is entailed on a distant male heir and cannot be sold, so she needs a proposal of marriage from her wealthy neighbour Edgar Caswall in order to gain financial security; 'but the good marriage on which she had fixed her eye did not seem to move quickly enough – indeed it did not seem to move at all – in the right direction.' (*LWW* 121) The other (supernatural) story that Stoker invents for her – through the eyes of his hero, Adam – is about men uncovering her secret and the filthy, corrupting primeval nature underneath which blights the whole district, and which must be destroyed before Adam can take possession of his inheritance. 'Such creatures may have grown up as well as down. They may have grown into or something like human beings. Lady Arabella March is of snake nature. She has committed crimes to our knowledge. She retains something of the vast strength of her primal being – can see in the dark – has the eyes of a snake....' (*LWW* 51). Inheritance within this framework is an important guarantor of one's identity – one's family, name or class. At the same time order is seen to be dependent on the woman being a reliable 'breeder' (to use Havelock Ellis' term), not a grotesque mutant hybrid.[39] It is for this reason that the heroes of *The Lair of the White Worm* return again and again to the stories and sites of previous generations and events, as indeed they do in other novels, the logic being that present-day mysteries about identity can only be solved by digging up the events of the past.

From the beginning of the novel, Arabella March is the source of the logical explanations which lie behind the text's seemingly fantastic events. She herself is a schemer and her plotting with Caswell and his black manservant, Oolonga, ensure that she is at the centre of the text's anxieties about class, inheritance and its wider fears about racial decay and degeneration. Arabella is a down-market version of the aristocrat; a grotesque parody of the aristocrat gone bad, one of those 'transformed human beings who had lost their humanity in some transformation or in the sweep of natural savagery' (*LWW* 287). Specifically aligned with what is regarded as the debased humanity of Oolonga, 'horrible distortion of a gentleman's servant' (*LWW* 37), 'a man hideously ugly, with the animal instincts developed in the lowest brutes; cruel, wanting in all the mental and moral faculties – in fact so brutal as to be hardly human' (*LWW* 36), it is seen as entirely natural that Arabella should put her services at the disposal of another predator, the hawk-like Caswell. He is another product of immoral or dysgenic practices, who has, in Darwinian terms, literally 'gone-ape', 'a cultured savage' and monomaniac. He is also a degenerate whose 'nature had become corrupted...all the baser...qualities had become more conspicuous' and whose family legacy of hypnotic power backfires, turning Edgar into the same zombie-like state that he intends for his victims (*LWW* 25; 105).[40] Behind this extraordinary picture of a diseased, immoral and degrading culture lies a counter image of an authentic aristocracy, 'the real heart of the old kingdom of Mercia', where men are men and women are women.

All these elements conspire in a fairly lurid way to make *The Lair of the White Worm* an exaggerated version of the works we have looked at so far. Other significant elements are also familiar. For instance, the story is written so as to enable the reader to watch Arabella (in the same way that the reader of *Dracula* is invited to track Lucy and Mina) and it offers a confusing glimpse into a side of her that the male characters are denied access to. Sometimes it seems as if the reader is meant to sympathize with her; she is 'plucky' and vulnerable (*LWW* 151). However, in the scenes that show Arabella plotting, she is revealed as a terrifying mixture of pure evil; 'fearsome' as one contemporary male reader told Stoker 'all impulsive emotionalism, rationality, cunning, sexual obsession'. A striking example of this is when she strips naked as she awaits the arrival of Caswall.[41] Rather like Dr Jekyll's house in Stevenson's *Dr Jekyll and Mr Hyde*, Arabella's house corresponds to herself; she tries to ensnare Adam by taking him through a series of locked doors, finally reaching the stinking basement which contains the gaping well hole. This heavy emphasis on 'phallic' snakes and cavernous openings is one of the reasons why the book has proved so enticing to psychoanalytic critics. One of the more convincing of these approaches is that offered by David Seed, where he suggests that it is difficult for the reader not to be sucked into reading the novel in this way and he notes how 'the gaping moist orifice depicts a fatal vaginal opening which dizzies Adam as he almost falls into the "charnel pit"'.[42]

However, this death trap is also part of a more general misogyny and sense of male panic existing within the text itself. The novel's interest in male psychology is revealed in the pronouncements made by Sir Nathaniel de Salis, the novel's Van Helsing figure and self-appointed expert on what women 'are'. The misogyny of his pronouncements – his comment for example that Arabella is a 'woman, with all a woman's wisdom and wit, combined with the heartlessness of a *cocotte* and the want of principle of a suffragette' has its origins in the polarized idea of woman as either Madonna or whore, as well as in fears about what the burgeoning Women's Suffrage Movement would do to men. Emmeline Pankhurst had formed the Women's Social and Political Union in 1903 and in 1911, the year of the novel's publication, the Union had began to step up its militant approach. ' "We may be sure", announces de Salis, "that in the fight before us there will be no semblance of fair play. Also that our unscrupulous opponent will not betray herself!" ' (*LWW* 143). Returning again and again to the spectre of Arabella March, the text is full of references to what women are supposed to be; the men try to locate her within the narrow parameters of middle-class sexual virtue and received wisdom relating to female sexuality. The scenes in which Arabella is shown scheming are also the means by which the novel suggests that she is more vulnerable (because 'feminine') than might first appear. Stoker shows her cowering from the unstable Caswell 'in a paroxysm of fear' (*LWW* 294). We also hear about Arabella's sexual frustration as a young woman, which – together with her apparent taste for killing – is attributed to a psychological disorder or nervous disturbance, one that, it is believed, her marriage will correct. A frustrated widow when the story opens, she must, Sir Nathaniel suggests, be possessed by some alien power, only 'that would explain the sudden revival of energy, the strange and inexplicable craving for maiming and killing'.

Although *The Lair of the White Worm* becomes Arabella March's story as much as it is Adam Salton's (there is a sense that Arabella begins to preoccupy Stoker rather more than he intended), the novel cannot imagine the reincorporation into society of a character whose criminality is as diverse and bloody as Arabella's. Her greatest act of villainy, however, is not the killing of the black manservant, Oolonga (within the indisputably ugly racist codes of the text, he is a lower-life form and so more or less expendable) but her plot with Edgar Caswell to ensnare Lilla, the defenceless 'girl of the Caucasian type, beautiful, Saxon, blonde' (*LWW* 36). It is for this reason that we get the fantasy resolution of the problem of the deadly woman: blown up by the resourceful hero when the well-hole – as we have seen, a possible symbol of the *vagina denta* – is packed with dynamite. Within the moral schema of the novel, we as readers, are supposed to be unperturbed by this and indeed to share in Adam's sense of relief as he listens to the 'agonised shrieks...rising [from the well-hole], growing ever more terrible with each second that passed....Once in a sort of lull or pause, the seething contents of the hole rose...and Adam saw part of the thin form of Lady Arabella, forced up to the top amid a mass of slime...' (*LWW* 316). In this way the deadly elements of the sexualized woman are turned back against her and the all important male identity, which depends on the control, if not the complete suppression of women, can be secured.

The violence of Lady Arabella's death by dismemberment, whilst it may provoke the reader's compassion, is thus structured to bring about narrative closure – a kind of grand finale in theatrical terms. As her body is blasted to bits, the narrative ends are tied together for the reader. And the potentially controversial aspects of the text – its having focused on the love of a black servant for a white female aristocrat – whilst not really resolved are exploded into nothingness. '["A]ll's well that ends well"' is how Adam and de Salis cheerfully put it, as they inspect the rotting pieces of the white worm, now covered with 'insects, worms and vermin of all kinds' before setting towards 'home' for a nice breakfast with Mimi. In this way the text positions the unresisting reader as 'satisfied' by Arabella's death: it also promises that we will not see her like again and that the future is in 'a new order of things', that is to say, the new family which will be created by Adam and Mimi. A final problem is, of course, the violent death of its problematic anti-heroine, which, when watched by the men, provides the reader with a disturbing closure to a troubling text.

In his working out of Arabella's destruction, the text poses for the reader some of the late-Victorian and Edwardian troubled attitudes to gender relations and the role of women; the idea that the serpent, being feminine 'will probably over reach herself' is deliberately controversial on Stoker's part, at the same time that it suggests his and culture's adherence to an entrenched set of ideas about gender roles. In suggesting the double-ness of Arabella and the virtues of Mimi ('strength of character' combined with 'sweetness of disposition') Stoker confirms not only his own but also his culture's expectations of women, only to expose them as unworkable. The confusions which are symbolized by the violent fragmentation of Arabella's body and the vigorous pushing of sexual desire underground, are those of the Edwardians more generally – the legacy of the chivalric idea and its underside and the rise of feminist issues which makes confrontation inevitable.

Like all of Stoker's novels, *The Lair of the White Worm* offers the reader a range of ideological positions and as twenty-first century readers we inevitably question some of them. The double focus on the white woman and the black servant as the novel's villains leaves the impression that there is a 'natural' link between them in some way, even if that link is the text's own sense of them as lesser beings. However, as I suggested in chapter 2, part of the interest of Stoker's texts is the way in which they seem revolutionary *and* reactionary at the same time, exposing the contradictions embedded within the ideologies of gender and race of their time. How far Stoker endorses these is a more complex question. In this chapter we have seen how the masculine situations or identities played out document some of the prejudices and anxieties held by many Victorian men at the *fin de siècle*. Stoker wrote too much on this for us not to think that he shared some of them. Nonetheless, there is another side to Stoker. As the discussion of *The Lair of the White Worm* suggests, in these same fictions Stoker is also concerned with the corresponding lives of women and it is this which can give Stoker's works a very different feel from other male writers of adventure romances. In the next chapter we will focus on this dimension of Stoker's writing and explore further the ways in which the texts engage with contemporary ideas of 'Woman' and the feminine.

4

Writing Women

In previous chapters I have looked at some of the ways in which
Stoker's novels deal with the invasion of the sacred English
home and the impact that this has on the lives of both male and
female characters. In this chapter, I will consider further how
Stoker's texts engage with the roles of women and their
assigned place in society, and how they represent the feminine.
Taking into account some of the historical changes that took
place between 1880 and 1910, I will try to reach conclusions
about the kinds of roles for women his writing seems to support.
Stoker deals with the position of women in almost all his works:
the choices women make, the pressure on them to 'act' in a
certain way, their transgressions from conventional standards of
behaviour, their sexuality and their relations with men. In this
chapter, however, I will focus on three novels that have received
little critical attention: *Miss Betty* (1898), *The Man* (1905) and the
multi-authored *The Fate of Fenella* (1891–2). I will also consider
three short stories which are collected in the posthumous
Dracula's Guest (1914), but which were written much earlier for
magazine publication: 'The Secret of the Growing Gold' (1892),
'The Squaw' (1893) and 'The Coming of Abel Behenna' (1914).
Stoker's short stories are often overlooked but they are
interesting in their own right and as texts that test some of the
themes, situations and characters and techniques that recur in
his full-length novels.

Contemporary reviewers of Stoker's fiction often saw his
novels as dealing at least in part with the 'Woman Question' or
what the turn-of-the-century sexologist Havelock Ellis later
described in *The Task of Social Hygiene* (1912) as the 'new culture
of woman...'.[1] In 1895, *The Morning Post*, in a review of the
adventure story *The Watter's Mou*, singled out Stoker's drowned

heroine Maggie (a name which carries echoes of Maggie Tulliver, the similarly fated heroine of George Eliot's *The Mill on the Floss* (1860) and the 'human tragedy' of her story for special comment, in particular 'the human interest offered by the struggle in the girl's soul and between the conflicting duties due to a father and lover'.[2] In 1898, a reviewer for the *North British Review* said something similar about *Miss Betty*, describing it as 'the story of a woman's devotion...'.[3] Although the novel was set in pre-Victorian times, it was written with a knowledge of what had happened in the years since and readers were invited to decide how much progress had been made in giving women more freedom, such as their rights to divorce and education. The female characters in *The Man* were also, as a reviewer for *The Bookman* noted in 1905, 'vividly conceived and drawn'. 'Mr Stoker is the master of the dramatic in fiction. And he has specially excelled in depicting this pure, delicately minded girl's nature...'[4]

From what we know of Stoker, he would seem an unlikely novelist to urge a more sympathetic understanding of women's role in society. As we have seen, he was by most accounts an outsize masculine figure, a good deal of whose life revolved around the male-dominated world of London's club-land. He could be extremely cautious, and in some cases reactionary, in his views of women's roles and responsibilities. Yet, in a chapter entitled 'Woman as Men', included in *Famous Impostors* – his penultimate book, published in 1910 – he writes admiringly of adventurous women who disguise themselves as men, and suggests that it is 'not to be wondered at' that there have been some women who, through the ages, have sought to rebel against conventional standards of behaviour. 'The legal and economic disabilities of the gentler sex stood then so fixedly in the way of working opportunity, that many women had no other choice.' Then, however, he downplays the radicalism of their behaviour explaining, in terms that would not have disgraced John Ruskin, that:

> In many of these cases are underlying romances, as of women making search for lost or absconding husbands, or of lovers making endeavours to regain the lost paradise of life together.
>
> If there were nothing else in these little histories, their perusal in detail would well repay attention as affording proof of the boundless

devotion of woman's love. No matter how badly the man may have treated the woman, no matter how heartlessly or badly he may have behaved towards her, her affection was proof against all. Indeed it makes one believe that there is some subtle self-sustaining, self-ennobling quality in womanhood which her initial self-surrender makes a constant force towards good. (*FI* 230–1)

This was not the first time Stoker had endorsed the essentialist models of femininity of the time in order to elaborate on the strengths and weaknesses of the 'gentler sex'. In a controversial talk on 'The Censorship of Fiction', given at the Authors' Club on 18 November 1907, he spoke out against the so-called 'sex problem' novel, a form of fiction 'that would be a disgrace to any country even less civilized than our own', written by authors who 'prostitute their talents' by knowingly exploiting the 'sex impulses' of their readership; 'a class of literature so vile that it is actually corrupting the nation'. He went on: 'The class of works to which I allude are meant by both authors and publishers to bring to the winning of commercial success the forces of inherent evil in man. The word man here stands for woman; indeed women are the worst offenders in this breach of moral law'. Here Stoker, who believed fiction to be 'the most powerful form of teaching available' to women, was not so much suggesting that women are inferior to or worse than men, merely that their innate sensibility and emotionalism makes them more impressionable readers and thus more likely to be corrupted, especially when the corruptors were, like Elinor Glyn, author of the steamy bestseller *Three Weeks* (1907), women themselves. Using analogies of sexual disease, contagion and addiction ('noxious drugs') he pointed out that the 'exposition of lewd suggestion' being offered to young women was defended on the grounds that it was tackling serious social problems, when – in his view – it was the fact that these works 'deal not merely with natural misdoing based on human weakness, frailty or passions of the senses, but with vices so flagitious, so opposed to even the decencies of human nature in its crudest and lowest forms, that the poignancy of moral disgust is lost in horror' (*CF* 484–5). The fervour of Stoker's condemnation was driven by his public-spirited, albeit con-servative, sense of the sexual mischief of these fictions, in which the anti-social behaviour exhibited by its women characters went not against political systems but against conventional (gender-based) standards of behaviour: the idealization of domesticity, home, the sanctity of marriage, female modesty and sexual purity, all of which played a crucial role in the institutional definition of women.

As we saw in chapter 1, some critics have suggested that this apparent ambivalence between Stoker's sympathetic awareness of the need to improve women's lives at the end of the nineteenth century, and the conservatism of some of his responses, has its origins in his relations with the women in his own family and social circle. The sense of his dynamic but domineering mother, Charlotte Stoker, as what Jane Gallop would term 'a phallic mother' whose monstrous influence was impossible to shake off, has lain behind a good many interpretations, as have the rumours of Florence's lack of interest in sex and her supposed inadequacies as a wife and mother.[5] Taken collectively and speculatively, the details of Stoker's relationships with these and other women – for example, the actresses Ellen Terry and Helen Barry – may suggest one reason why the idea of the family, domesticity and of women's role within these spaces forms such an important part of Stoker's work; they represent a kind of therapeutic writing out of a complicated private life.

But a biographical explanation of Stoker's work should not mean that we ignore other contexts or dehistoricize it. His portrayal of women in his fictions may have been particular to him but it also drew on other available conventions and contexts. As we have seen, the last decades of the nineteenth century saw great changes in women's lives, the effects of which have been the subjects of important scholarship by (amongst others) Lyn Pykett, Sally Ledger and Ann Heilmann.[6] The resurgence of the 'Woman Question' in the 1890s, including questions and viewpoints about female emancipation (legal, financial, domestic), about a woman's ability to make her own decisions, her right to vote, her right to be able to petition for custody of her legitimate children, were seen as threats to the presumed stability of Victorian and Edwardian patriarchal culture. As Lynda Nead has noted, the construction of the 'separate spheres' ideology around which so much of Victorian society had been founded 'was part of a wider formation of class identity, nation and empire....International leadership and the domination of foreign competition were believed to depend directly on the existence of a stable domestic base and social stability.'[7] But by the 1880s there was a feeling that modern woman, was as Lyn Pykett puts it, 'in flight from motherhood, family responsibility and domestic existence.'[8] The response of many people to what the theatre critic, Clement Scott writing in 1891, called the 'de-sexed...the unwomanly, the unsexed females, the whole army of unprepossessing cranks in petti-coats...educated and much ferreting dogs...effeminate men and male women'[9] was to try to prevent women from deviating from existing moral codes and seek to re-contain them in a more domestic definition, a pre-lapsarian view of women and one which sustained hard-won masculine identity.

As students of late-Victorian and Edwardian fiction, we do not have to travel very far to realize just how far novelists of the time were preoccupied with the issue of 'woman': the 'monstrous' woman, the 'erotomaniac', the emancipated woman who committed the cardinal sin of 'unsexing' herself by personally rejecting marriage and sacred motherhood alto-gether. So whilst Stoker's own personal experience of women can be useful in shedding light on his fiction, the discussion which follows will suggest some of the ways in which Stoker's fictions draw on, and engage with, some of these models, character types and plots, as well as with other discourses of the 1890s and 1900s – medical, social, racial – about womanhood, femininity and the feminine, which formed part of a wider uncertainty about modern identities. It is striking, for example, how in texts like *Dracula* and *Miss Betty* Stoker seems to adopt a conservative male gendered stance with the result that his interest in women in society is one that we have no difficulty in labelling 'patriarchal'. In other works discussed in this book – *The Snake's Pass, The Lair of the White Worm* and *The Lady of the Shroud*, these markers of an ideal conventional femininity form an important touchstone for the novel's men. Yet whilst Stoker does not offer an explicitly feminist critique of his society in the way that, for example, outspoken women writers of the 1890s such as George Egerton or Mona Caird do, it is difficult to read Stoker's work without noticing that he is clearly interested in the underside of domesticity, in the darker workings within the family, in female lives lived in a male-dominated society, and the indoctrination and victimization which this may involve.

THE FATE OF FENELLA

Often ignored as a literary curiosity, *The Fate of Fenella* provides a useful starting point for seeing how the simultaneity of these various positions exist in practice and it brings to the fore many of the concerns played out in Stoker's other works, including his rather ambivalent relation to issues of gender and female subjectivity. Advertized in 1891 as an experimental novel, *The Fate of Fenella* was also something of a literary gimmick, 'a curiosity of collaboration' and 'a curious mosaic'[10] as reviewers described it, with each chapter being written by twenty-four different novelists (including such popular late-Victorian names as Arthur Conan Doyle, Florence Marryat and Helen Mathers), passed along from one to the other before being serialized in weekly instalments in *The Gentlewoman* (29 November 1891– 7 May 1892). The domesticated and 'feminine' accents of this magazine, with its emphasis on fashion and household tips, are not ones that we immediately connect with Bram Stoker; as we have seen, he was often read (and liked to be read) primarily as a figure of gentlemanly masculine culture. But by 1891, Stoker was beginning to establish his value as a professional author for hire within the world of magazine fiction, and was improving his ability to manipulate the language and tenor of his stories to suit particular audiences. For an ambitious writer, the chance to collaborate with a host of other better-known novelists, also offered the chance to gain a certain lustre by association, something that, as Stoker's detractors pointed out, he was always wont to do.

Generically, *The Fate of Fenella* can be labelled a 'sensation novel' and invites comparison with kinds of fiction made famous by such writers as Wilkie Collins, Mary Braddon and Ellen (Mrs Henry) Wood in the 1860s and 1870s. This was a provocative form of fiction, which took its title from the contemporary theatre's 'sensation drama', and drew on the techniques of popular melodrama and newspaper reports of criminal trials in order to bring murder, adultery, bigamy, illegitimacy, madness and sexual deviance into the confines of the respectable middle or upper-class drawing room. In *The Fate of Fenella*, the world of Fenella Ffrench falls apart when her lover, the Austrian Count de Murger, is found stabbed to death in Fenella's hotel room in Harrogate and she is charged with his murder. The murderer is actually Fenella's estranged husband, Lord Frank Onslow who kills the Count in a 'hypnotic trance' (*FF* II 11). Unable to bear the thought of his wife's adultery, Frank leaves England unaware of his part in the Count's death, while Fenella is defended at her trial (a 'hideous nightmare' (*FF* I 23) by Clitheroe Jacynth who is both barrister and admirer, and who persuades the excited jury that Fenella, believing that she was going to be raped, killed the Count in 'justifiable' self-defence in protection of her 'honour' (*FF* II 11). Although she is acquitted, the 'stain' upon Fenella's character means that she is shunned by 'respectable' society. It also means that she is judged an unfit mother for her young son, Ronnie. Whilst technically a 'free woman', 'the laws of her country [having]... given her back her liberty' (*FF* I 231), she is forced to leave England and inhabit a kind of subterranean existence, taking on the role of what is 'other', subversive and marginal. The total effect of all this is to remind readers that Fenella's disruptive femininity is a thing to be shunned because it is a threat to conventional standards of behaviour.

One of the ways in which *The Fate of Fenella* is useful for understanding something of Stoker's position on the 'Woman Question' is that it gives us an opportunity to place Stoker's ideas about woman and the feminine alongside those of some of his contemporaries. Because this is a multi-authored novel there are lots of different voices vying for our attention. The result is a narrative which, as Lillian Nayder puts it, is deliberately 'teasing and playful': 'the contributors...challenging each other with unexpected and bizarre twists and turns in the plotline', also undermining, in some cases, the moral message that has gone before. Interspersed with these various voices is a debate about gender, marriage and domesticity but one that is 'necessarily open-ended' and 'divided'.[11]

Stoker's characteristically energetic chapter 'Lord Castleton Explains' (chapter 10) forms part of the middle section of the novel. It focuses on Fenella's exile and is striking for its inscription of some of the anxieties he and his society sometimes felt in regard to transgressive women. Not least of these anxieties is the figuring of the unruly woman as a dangerous presence, one troublesome to the stability of the social structure presided over by men. For Lord Onslow and his friend, Lord Castleton, Fenella's very notoriety is, of course, a sign that she is no better than she should be. In contrast, the story of Clitheroe Jacynth's sister, Helen Grandison, reminds us that respectable women have no story, they stand quietly in their proper place on the side-lines of the action. So while Stoker describes how the trial has 'softened' Fenella, he also has her husband's close friend, Lord Castleton, cast doubt on Fenella's brave display of 'wifely devotion' in shielding her husband from a charge of murder. Far from being a heroine, Castleton believes that Fenella is no better than she should be, that she took the blame for her husband's crime to cover up a more horrible crime: her own adultery. 'Where, then', asks Lord Castleton, 'was Fenella's heroism after all?':

> [S]he had taken the blame on herself; but might it not have been that she was morally guilty all the same? Why then had she taken the blame? Was it not because she feared that her husband might have refused to screen her shame; or that she feared that if any less heroic aspect of the tragedy were presented to the public, her own fair fame might suffer in greater degree? Could it be that Fenella Onslow was not a heroine, only a calculating woman of exceeding smartness? (*FF* II 25–6)

Within the context of the novel, Lord Castleton's dismissive reaction to Fenella's self-sacrifice illustrates the misogyny inherent in the ways in which men respond to women. Fenella falls and hence becomes a threat to the stability of society, a society based on the control of women's sexuality. She is presented by Stoker – without apparent irony – as a sexually-compromised woman. To the serial's female readers there could hardly be a stronger deterrent to transgressing than the misery which informs the disgraced Fenella's sense of herself as an outcast, sent 'mad' with shame before collapsing into a near-fatal attack of brain fever. This, together with Stoker's comments on 'the protective feeling which is part of a woman's love' (*FF* II 4–5), makes it possible for the novel to be interpreted as a discourse on the process of constructing gender identities and

107

the binary oppositions which sustain them. Surrounded as he was in the pages of *The Fate of Fenella* by a number of 'New Woman' writers, Stoker depicts the stereotype of the unruly woman with a degree of distaste, while at the same time positioning the heroine so that we feel some sympathy for her, particularly in light of the entrenched male attitudes she is up against. He and the other novelists position us as readers so that we become voyeuristic spectators of Fenella's misery.

The second part of *The Fate of Fenella* stresses the kinds of negotiations that any woman might be expected to undertake in order to meet society's expectations. Most of the contributors use the heroine's enforced separation from her son, and her solitary exile under a false name, to rehearse a fairly predictable idealization of motherhood and female passivity:

> He had spoken to her of her boy, and the cold emptiness of her heart ached with the sudden rush of emotion as she cried out, with outstretched arms: 'My boy! Bring me my boy!' To press the child in her arms, to feel the soft down of his cheek against hers to hear the lisping 'Muzzer, muzzer dear!' from his lips, to have his arms around her – this, this would save her reason. She felt her reason going, felt her mind darkened, the path before her no longer clear (*FF* II 85).

Fenella's punishment and her resulting hysteria is an upper-class version of the fate that befalls the majority of 'fallen' women in nineteenth-century fiction – intended to serve as a powerful lesson in the necessity of self-control and of accepting things as they are. More striking than this, however, is the way in which the novel reveals how masculine structures, which depend in part on the subjugation of women, are made possible. When it comes to keeping Fenella in her proper place, ideological inscription is supplemented by male coercion – revealed as a less physical but no less effective version of the staking of Lucy Westenra in *Dracula* – and by a powerful display of masculine moral superiority – of the kind Stoker would also later deploy in *The Lair of the White Worm*. Seen in this light, feminist critics might argue that the novel can be read as an exposé of the way in which a patriarchal society manages to keep women in a slave-like position at the same time as fostering in them the belief that their own desires are sinful and in need of policing. Fenella is transported off to Guernsey, given a small allowance and separated from her son ('for his own good') by the novel's stock chivalric figure, Clitheroe Jacynth, in order that she does not further 'stain' her son's and her husband's lives. Not only has she forfeited any chance of gaining a place in 'respectable' society but also she is no longer deemed a fit nurturer of children. Heartbroken, Fenella has destroyed, she believes, her very reason for being, her very 'self'.

Throughout the novel Fenella is described as a woman of impulse 'and recklessness' (*FF* I 50) and this cannot go unchecked. The novel's authors show how destructive Fenella's undisciplined behaviour is to her happiness and it is only by reining in this tendency that she achieves contentment. There is a sense of *déjà vu* about the final chapters, which detail Fenella's decline into a life-threatening collapse and illness. Hers is the kind of conveniently vague illness that many Victorian novelists found so useful. Fenella herself may become incoherent but her own story is actually very tidy. She emerges from her illness with a restored identity created by her realization of the possibilities inherent in being 'a happy wife and mother' (*FF* II 103). Seen in this light *The Fate of Fenella* is escapist but it also propagates a number of ideological messages. Alongside the condemnation of upper-class excess, it is most obviously a text designed to remind its female readers of their social responsibilities, of the joys and privileges of motherhood and of the fact that motherhood is woman's primary duty as a citizen. Simplicity, self-abnegation, nurturing, passivity, these are touchstones of Fenella's new 'feminine nature', rather than the insensate love of pleasure which characterizes her at the beginning of the novel. So, whilst the serial is suffused with chapters where readers are invited to question the various punishments meted out to the heroine, these narratives are, as in the later novel, *Miss Betty*, constantly elbowed out of the way by a more conventional preoccupation with 'women's sphere' on the part of Stoker and the novel's more conservative contributors.

MISS BETTY

The historical novel, *Miss Betty*, is one of the least-known of Stoker's novels but, of all his works, it was the one that provoked the most enthusiastic response from reviewers when first published. 'A delightful surprise' was how the *Bookman* described it: 'From *Dracula* to *Miss Betty* is such a far cry that it is almost impossible to realize that both novels come from the same pen. *Miss Betty* is exactly the soothing, quiet, "pretty" novel to read after a day spent in the company of harrowing problematists. It is one of those simply-told idyllic love stories which are now so out of fashion and which come as a boon and a blessing to restore one's faded faith in fiction.'[12] What made the tale so seductive to critics was its blatant appeal to the romance of 'Heritage' and the textualization of the myth of 'olde England' that became something of a national pursuit in the 1890s. Stoker tells his story in a tone of nostalgia that struck a chord with contemporary reviewers and restored his standing with reviewers who had shuddered at *Dracula*. The *North British Daily News* wrote approvingly that:

> Mr Stoker is evidently determined to demonstrate to the world his power over the softer emotions as well as over the repulsive and horrible for nothing can be imagined more antithetical to the creepy 'Dracula' than...a delightful portrait of an old charm of romance and naiveté of expression... If this volume is a fair sample of what 'Latter Day' stories are going to be then we cannot too highly congratulate the publishers in the exceptional literary quality of their new series.[13]

As an example of 1890s historical fiction, *Miss Betty* has many of the outward features of this hugely popular sub-genre. It seems reactionary and glorifies the national past using reminders of a lost 'golden age' as an ideological weapon in the struggles of the present day. In the troubled 1890s the appeal of such writing seemed obvious. As Len Platt notes: 'Here an idealized version of culture and society could be preserved. Class conflict could be erased, traditional gender roles maintained, and true distinction distinguished from any vulgar or oppressive exercise of power and privilege.'[14] The quietness, 'charm', repose and 'limpid delicacy of effect' that contemporary critics valued in *Miss Betty* derived largely from this promise of a more tranquil, seemingly less-confusing world, where the aggressive 'she animal' of modern times had been replaced by a sweeter, more obviously 'winsome' heroine.[15]

The diminutive orphan Betty Pole, as the novel's title makes clear, is at the centre of the story. A representative of young womanhood, she is also a pertinent example of the way in which, in historical fiction, history tends to be seen through the struggles of a tiny minority who are forced to make judgments and decisions. *Miss Betty* is a love story but, like *Dracula*, it is also about the threats to the stability and order of the English family unit posed by outsiders. Miss Betty's fortune and its attendant responsibilities are bequeathed to her by her great-grandfather (a heroic supporter of Charles I at the time of the English Civil War) as an act of faith in her abilities to carry on the honourable traditions of the family. In the 'political unconscious' of the novel (to use Fredric Jameson's much-quoted phrase[16]) Betty's inheritance of the money also signifies the unavoidable and all-encompassing legacy of longstanding English traditions of loyalty, patriotism, family and duty. Even young women are enlisted in the roll call of service stemming back to the time of Betty's namesake, Elizabeth I. As her great-grandfather tells her: 'All the faces I have loved seem to gather in yours tonight. The face of my mother, who when a child like you stood with her mother on the heights of Portland Bill and saw the great Armada sweep in the channel' (*MB* 17–18). The novel tries to perform the ideological function of constructing from personal life histories a larger history of the English nation and of the role played in it by women.

The penniless Rafe Otwell's rescue of Betty from the Thames, his subsequent courtship, his secret identity as a highwayman and his lavish presents to Betty, notably a large Indian ruby, prompt the central 'mystery' around which the plot is constructed. Rafe is shown to be in thrall to his kinsman, the vampiric Robert Walpole who wants him to make a marital alliance with an elderly heiress. Economically dependent on his relation, Rafe has 'a sort of feeling that Sir Robert had him in his power and meant to mould him to his will (*MB* 88). To escape Walpole's predatory clutches he becomes a highwayman (a role equally as predatory) robbing payroll shipments on deserted roads, rather than borrow the money from Betty. In this sense it is Rafe's response to his dilemma (and Betty's ignorance of his dilemma), which propels the plot. For Betty the mystery of the ruby – the jewel – becomes wrapped up with questions of Rafe's behaviour. Literally and figuratively, Rafe goes missing – via his long absences, his entanglement with Walpole, his disguises and the new personalities he tries on. He moves in and out of different contemporary identities in the novel to become the mystery, the rescue to be effected, the priceless object to be restored to the novel's heroine.

Rafe himself is a rather unimpressive character in the book as a whole and is by no means as memorable as Sir Robert Walpole, who is powerfully, if melodramatically brought to life by Stoker. In Rafe's case, Stoker's main interest is in someone who is tempted to take the easy way out. In proposing to Betty he is making the right choice; in resisting the villainous Walpole 'now the virtual ruler of England' and refusing to let Betty help him with money he displays the right 'masculine pride'. But he is also reckless and irresponsible and not destined to get very far by honest hard work, as society now demands (England is now a bustling mercantile society). His role as a highwayman represents his tendency to run away from realities. In contrast, in Betty, the reader is introduced to that combination of female purity and honesty which Stoker used in his representation of Mina Harker, another character who seems to conform to the different cultural identities provided by families and society. A lengthy study could be made of Stoker's controlling use of diminutives in *Miss Betty*. Betty's 'direct simplicity', her 'sweetness', her feminine modesty and Christianity makes her attractive (in Rafe's eyes) and governs her everyday conduct, including her falling in love with Rafe. Her behaviour, the narrator tells his readers, holds true for all women. Love is, he explains:

> ...latent only until such time as true attachment manifests itself, whereupon it asserts all its strength...like all great forces, what it loses in strength it gains in direction and *vice versa*. For the timorous young maiden when she feels assured that her lover holds back through some strange weakness which is alien to feminine nature – and her heart never fails to tell her when this is so – takes heart of grace and gives freely if not ostentatiously, that which timid self consciousness fears even to ask. (*MB* 43–4)

The didactic element in *Miss Betty* is perhaps more evident here than anywhere else. The moment is deliberately reminiscent of the conduct book but it can also be read as a response to contemporary anxieties about womanhood. Faced with 'The Revolt of the Daughters' (the title of Blanche Althea Crackenthorpe's controversial 1894 article in the *Nineteenth Century*), Stoker gives his readers not the animalistic, 'masculine' and forward 'New Woman' but a woman whose feelings are in line with older conventional models of feminine feeling. In the extract cited previously, Rafe Otwell has declared his love to Betty and she reciprocates it. Her conventional view of love places all responsibility for her declaration on the man, while the woman remains dormant until such desire is awakened in her. But once such passion has been set free she may show it, as she does, through fidelity and dedication.

It is in this way that we see Stoker contributing to the cultural construction of a popular nostalgia-tinged version of English womanhood prevalent in the 1890s, an appeal legitimized by contemporary reviewers of the novel who believed, as a writer for the *St James Budget* put it in 1894, that 'The public who read to kill time are getting heartily sick of squalor and the she animal.'[17] For the *North British Review*, cited earlier, the interest of *Miss Betty* lay not in any exploration of self-serving patriarchy or garish expression of *fin de siècle* fears but rather as a statement of a bygone era characterized by elegance and order where everyone (i.e. servants and women) knew their place. This is an important ideological function of Stoker's novel: to stabilize and maintain the cultural meaning of woman – passive, nurturing, responsive and one which helps explain the 'normalization' of Stoker's take on womanhood, which appears in contemporary reviews.

Miss Betty can fruitfully be read, then, as a conservative text. But it carries another, perhaps more liberating, message. Like many historical romances, the text is escapist, offering women readers the possibilities of (sexual) adventure with swashbuckling heroes (Rafe Otwell, 'a handsome young fellow with black hair and dark eyes and a proud bearing'). At the same time, Stoker's representation of Betty demonstrates his tendency to applaud female initiative and independent action, qualities that we also see in texts like *The Watter's Mou*, *The Lady of the Shroud* and *Lady Athlyne*. The second half of the narrative is driven by Betty's determination to assume (secretly) the role of detective, keeping her own counsel, her 'course of thought...masked by her habitual direct simplicity' (*MB* 44). Betty's attempts to track down Rafe – riding alone on the open road in order to try to catch him in the act of robbery – carry with them danger as well

113

as pleasure. In this sense, Stoker's historical novel might also be seen to be offering women the kind of 'escapist fantasy' described by Alison Light in her study of women and historical fiction, whereby 'heroines are able to take up what would usually be seen as the masculine reins of power and sexual autonomy'.[18] In Stoker's case, of course, he makes it very clear – whilst hinting at the possibilities for adventure and self-fulfilment for women outside the home – that Betty's actions are dictated by her desire to save Rafe. By doing so, he announces her suitability for the much commended role of self-sacrificing and redeeming Victorian angel: 'unworthy, though he had proved, she loved him still; and, as even he had given life to her, so if need be should that life be given for him in return' (*MB* 95).

That said, it is not very difficult to see that Betty's real secret, which provides the basis for the most important personal conflict in the novel, is that her love for Rafe is sexual as well as spiritual. That she desires Rafe might thus be read as a mark of subversion, in the sense that, firstly, he is undesirable as a suitor and, secondly, that it is the passive, feminine woman who is doing the desiring. The entire novel is suffused with images that suggest ways in which her self-containment masks an inward struggle to resolve complex choices of sexuality, morality and way of life and the somewhat masochistic self-repression in the name of duty, which is often assumed to be typically Victorian. After one meeting with Rafe, she watches him go 'standing still as if carved out of stone. The red glare of the sunset fell full upon her smiting her pale face and snowy garments till from head to foot she looked as if dipped in blood' (*MB* 122). While she joins in the hunt for Rafe, Betty is also engaged in a search of her own, uncovering, and then coming to terms with, what she recognizes as the truth about herself, that: 'she...glorified in the strength and daring of her lover, in his rapid action and the vigour of his determination'; and 'womanlike she felt happy because the man was strong' (*MB* 157). Worthless and idle as he is, Rafe acts as the prime mover in Betty's recognition of her own desires.

Yet this vision of a young woman in search of her sexual self is, as elsewhere in Stoker's texts, counter-pointed by a sense of shame and fear. This is exemplified in a scene where the heroine, knowing that her lover is in the next room, contemplates herself in the mirror:

Betty looking out straight in front of her, saw her image in the tall mirror. She dared not stir; she might not venture even to put a sheltering hand before her burning face lest the rustling of her dress should betray her presences. It seemed to her that listening as she was in secret it was almost immodest to behold even her own image in the glass and so closed her eyes – and listened. She heard Rafe sob, and each word went beating through her heart like the throb of a giant pulse. (*MB* 174)

This spectacle of the heroine's feelings and sensations at a moment of crisis – is the source of the novel's most sensational writing. As a spectacle of awakening sexuality, it is both complex and poignant. This is largely because the heroine cannot voice what she feels. Nor is it an accident that the novel's most consistent imagery is that which shows Betty against the natural settings of rural England, hinting at the antipathy between so-called 'civilized' behaviour and her natural emotions. The climactic example of this occurs in chapter 10, in which Betty prepares to confront Rafe in his guise of highwayman. In this scene of personal ordeal, set on a deserted road surrounded by dense woodland, Stoker extends the image of a mortal facing personal cataclysm to include crypto-religious symbols. These help reinforce the image of the heroine as a woman striving to effect a scheme of personal destiny. The artificial is left behind:

For she had two hearts now. One which was full of pain and weariness, for which life had all gone by and which was but like the ash of an extinct fire, with naught remaining but sentience and the power to suffer pain. The other heart was new and fresh – such a heart as might be in the breath of one who had been born again in a new and higher life. The roads were dusty, and the sun glared fiercely as the moon drew night. The trees and grass were losing the freshness of their green; but there were places of deep shadow where the trees arched over the roadway and there were many purling trills which made music cool and sweet as the waters gurgled in the chasms of their stony bed or flashed as they fell. (*MB* 136–7)

This passage, with its heightened language, is another rich example of Stoker's pantheistic invocation of the natural landscape used – as we saw earlier in *The Snake's Pass* and *The Lady of the Shroud* – to convey a sense of his protagonist's inner feelings. In this instance, Stoker exploits the association of femininity with feeling but also suggests a woman who has chosen to descend not only into the deserted landscape of the countryside but also to venture into the unexplored terrain of her own mind. Betty's travels on the deserted road parallel her current withdrawals into self, in order to search for other courses of action but also represent an awakening, something evident in the mystical or religious overtones of the passage. The reference to the two hearts reminds us that this is a novel of moral and emotional pilgrimage.

But if *Miss Betty* can be seen as a meditation on female subjectivity and selfhood on one level, it nevertheless resolves matters conventionally, if not altogether unambiguously, in favour of Betty and Rafe's marriage at a time when, as Jeffrey Weeks argues, 'socialization' was a 'determining notion' and marriage still its 'social cement'.[19] When Betty confronts Rafe he leaves the country to escape hanging and does penance, spending a year as a Turkish galley slave. Betty waits for him and five years later, he returns from exile, resurrected and rich with the spoils of war, 'the nobler part of the soul within stood revealed without dross' (*MB* 185). What he lacked before – money and patriotism – he now has in abundance and this puts him on a more equal footing with Betty and enables them to marry. In the meantime, having 'saved' Rafe, Betty has relinquished her assertiveness ready to assume willingly the role of wife. This is perhaps a lightweight ending for a novel in which so much emphasis is placed on the heroine's *bildung*. Overall, though, the process of Rafe's painfully-won redemption – the way in which his dissident, anti-social behaviour is replaced by an increasingly publicly and patriotically-minded lifestyle in the British army – strengthens the structure and moral content of the novel by moving in parallel to Betty's experiences. There is a greater emphasis than before on the importance of personal integrity in forming relationships. The novel's quest-like narrative closes with characters who embody the values dear to Stoker: belief in personal relationships, in honesty, in feeling, in bravery.

THE MAN

In *The Second Sex*, Simone de Beauvoir wrote that 'one is not born a woman, one becomes one'. De Beauvoir's point behind her much quoted comment was that ' "woman" is a "cultural construction", rather than a biological one'. As Ruth Robbins notes, the reason why this remark is so important is that it highlights the fact that 'the ideas about male and female roles which any given society may have come to regard as natural are not really so, and that given that they are not natural, they may even be changed'.[20] De Beauvoir's insight is a useful starting point for a discussion of *The Man*. Like *Miss Betty*, this novel takes the construction of the feminine as its central concern. Stoker's interest, however, is very obviously in the way in which women's supposed weakness is culturally enforced. The boundaries at issue are the distinctions between men and women, the 'separate spheres' of their existence and what happens when women actively question the construction of gender.

Outwardly the story is a simple one: the unusually-named Stephen Norman, a beautiful, orphaned heiress, questions the conventional restrictions on female behaviour, believing that women should be allowed rights and privileges equal to those enjoyed by men. She is involved with two men: the handsome but profligate Leonard Everard, and another childhood friend, the reliable Harold An Wolf. With 'the vague desires of budding womanhood trembling within her' Stephen proposes marriage to Leonard but he rejects her and compounds Stephen's sense of shame by trying to blackmail her (*M* 105–6). Stephen is contemplating how to get over this when Harold, having previously taken on the role of Stephen's father/brother/teacher, feels protective of her and this, combined with latent sexual attraction and jealousy of Leonard, leads him to make his own proposal to her. In an angry altercation, she refuses him. ' "You thought, I suppose" ' she tells him, ' "that this poor, neglected, despised, rejected woman, who wanted so much to marry that she couldn't wait for a man to ask her, would hand herself over to the first chance newcomer who threw his handkerchief to her; would hand over herself and her fortune!" ' (*M* 185). The revelation of Stephen as 'not angelic but human' tempered with

117

her heinous proposal to Leonard and her dismissal of him, is a horrible shock to Harold's system, destroying all his illusions about women and himself. Expelled from Stephen's life and story, Harold goes off to seek his fortune in Alaska. The narrative then speeds forward two years, bringing the action of the book up to the turn of the century. Harold returns to England, only to be shipwrecked off the coast of that part of England where Stephen, now Lady de Lannoy, lives. Blinded in the wreck, he lies unrecognizable in Stephen's home under her care. The novel closes as Stephen, now more 'feminine' and having discovered Harold's real identity agrees to marry him. The novel's preoccupation with identities (gender, racial, class, sexual) is apparent in its powerfully allusive title. At the literal level, the title refers to Harold An Wolf, a recognizable macho Stoker-type but it also refers to Stephen's modern attempts to move out of the female sphere and to assume the roles and responsibilities traditionally associated with men, whilst in Stephen's lonely heart, it also comes to stand for the mate she is trying to find – a title she bestows on Leonard.

If we examine the novel closely, it is not difficult to appreciate why some contemporary reviewers should have seen *The Man* as a reprisal of 'New Woman' fiction; a genre notorious in the 1890s, as Ann Heilmann has noted, for depicting 'female sexual autonomy, linked to an attack on, or rejection of, male sexual practice.'[21] It is self-consciously constructed as a novel of sexual confusion and claims a place in the literature of 'sexual anarchy' (to use George Gissing's evocative description of the *fin de siècle*). It is a story of sexual awakening on the part of a woman with a man's name; in Stephen we encounter a woman who wants to develop 'masculine' skills, who has, one contemporary reviewer noted, 'a romantic and dangerous belief in the equality of the sexes'[22] and who, like lots of other New Women heroines, takes the unwarranted step of making the first move on a man.

Like the earlier novels *The Fate of Fenella*, *Dracula* and *Miss Betty*, *The Man* is about the choices open to women, what they want (or think they want) and the kind of behaviour they exhibit while trying to get it. Stephen Norman, described by Stoker as possessing 'remarkable promise of splendid womanhood' (*M* 3), is the character in this story who stands out most as a representative of assertive modern womanhood but there are a number of other important kinds of women in the novel. These include Mrs Egerton, a lecturer and political activist at the women-only Somerville College, Oxford (whose name is presumably meant to remind us of the well-known New Woman writer, George Egerton) and whose charity work among the poor, the 'submerged tenth' of the East End (*M* 88), Stephen sees at first hand. There is also Susan Mingis, an ambitious working-class girl who, seduced and 'flung [away]...like a broken toy' (*M* 111) by her gentleman lover (later revealed to be Leonard), drowns herself in the River Thames. Finally, there is Laetitia Rowley, Stephen's unmarried aunt, who accepts her domestic role, silently enduring 'the self-repressions which go to make up the habit of a well-bred woman' but is unfulfilled. It is Stephen's relationship with the latter which provides the basis for most of the text's debates and the most important point of contrast between Stephen and her aunt lies in their ideas about relations between the sexes. Stephen is described as an 'up-to-date twentieth-century girl' (*M* 120); Laetitia Rowley is a well-bred Victorian spinster. She has no doubt about what women ought to do. However, her views on the importance of social rules clearly belong to a older tradition, 'knit in the very fibres of her being by the remorseless etiquette of a thousand years', a position which in Stephen's eyes seems destructive to women's happiness (*M* 133). In contrast, Stephen's habits of mind and expression – her question 'Why should one be mute?' (*M* 91) – belong to a more modern outlook.

What is interesting about this novel is its recognition that women might want something more than domesticity. *The Man* is full of references to what women are, and are supposed to be and Stoker's depiction of Stephen Norman's struggle for something to 'do' directly addresses the kinds of complaints made by his more obviously feminist contemporaries, who pleaded with mothers not to keep their daughters in ignorance and to give them the freedom to make their own decisions. Alys W. Pearsall Smith wrote in the *Nineteenth Century* of 'unmarried girls slowly but surely withering in ideas and interests' who are forced to 'crush back the aspirations of their own natures, and must stifle the cry of their own individuality.'[23] Stephen Norman tries to rebel against the life-denying adherence to conventionality that Miss Rowley has locked herself into and, in this respect, Stoker encapsulates much of what New Woman writers were saying about the suppression of women's speech and desires. '[T]he forces of life allocated to a woman were closing in on her; and naturally enough her dominant nature rebelled. All the little self-repressions which go to make up the habit of a well-bred woman became irksome to her.' (*M* 70) Her sex and her status place her, she is told, outside the possibility of direct action. Although Stephen is a landowner, the idea of attending the local court is deemed quite inappropriate since it involves her listening to ' "low people speaking of low crimes, cases of a kind' that she is 'not supposed to know anything about" ' (*M* 83). Later, in the same exchange, Stephen, annoyed by what she regards as her aunt's mindless parroting of the current received wisdom of 'separate spheres', harangues her on the subject of the sexual double-standard, i.e. what her aunt describes as: 'The sin, my dear, of woman's wrong doing....as woman...of mother-hood, without marriage!':

> All Stephen's nature seemed to rise in revolt....'You speak of a woman's wrongdoing, when surely it is a man's as well. There does not seem to be blame for him who is the more guilty. Only for poor women!...And Auntie dear, it is such poor women that I should like to help...Not when it is too late but before! But how can I help unless I know? Good girls cannot tell me, and good women won't! You yourself, Auntie didn't want to speak on the subject; even to me!'
>
> And as she spoke she looked glorified. The afternoon autumn sun shone full through the great window and lightened her up till she looked like a spirit. Lighted her white diaphanous dress till it seemed to take shape as an ethereal robe; lighted her red hair till it looked like a celestial crown; lighted her great dark eyes till their black beauty became sweet in the tide of glory. (*M* 86–7)

It seems clear that at some level, Stoker was persuaded by contemporary feminist arguments about the need for women to be given the same educational, political and social opportunities as men. Steven's opinions about 'fallen men' also have a good deal in common with the controversial suffragist slogan 'Votes for Women, Purity for Men', a stance which was supported by social purity feminists and by those 'New Woman' writers who used powerful images of female victimization and male sexual misconduct as a way of suggesting contemporary man's unfitness for marriage. One of these men is Leonard Everard:

effete, delicate, 'essentially a voluptuary', a far cry from the examples of tough masculinity we saw in the previous chapter. A 'pretty boy with blue eyes and curly light brown hair', a figure well-fashioned and alert', 'movements...light and graceful as a young fawn', he is ornamental, 'good to look upon' but is presented in the text via language which conveys languorous effeminacy rather than energetic butch virility (*M* 41). Rather like Wilde's Dorian Gray, his appearance betrays no hint of the truth, namely, that Leonard is one of Stoker's social villains; a serial seducer driven on in pursuit of self-gratification, with 'no qualms or scruples in a matter of gratifying his own desires' (*M* 42). He is clearly antithetical to Stephen, not least because he is a bastion of male values in which the process of education has worked almost too well: 'an egotist, and the very incarnation of selfishness...a prig of the first water. He had been raised altogether in convention.' (*M* 132) 'Home', Leonard believes, 'was the proper place for girls, looking after things, and playing croquet and tennis – when they were wanted to play' and he takes pleasure in his knowing how to 'use the whip with the weaker sex' (*M* 150; 260). Leonard is clearly embarrassed by, and uncomprehending of, Stephen's presumption in proposing to him, unable to believe anything other than that a woman should be ornamental and silent – and that a husband should rule a wife.

Leonard's stance as a kind of spokesman for all men means that any idea that Stephen can single-handedly push events in a different direction emerges as unrealistic, even dangerous. Nonetheless, Stoker presents Stephen's strength of feeling as attractive – certainly more attractive than Leonard's chauvinism. Elsewhere, Miss Rowley's position as a moral reference point also seems much less secure. Even as she clings onto her pious principles of feminine repression – principles which some of Stoker's readers would have accepted as right and proper – these readers are being asked to identify with and admire Stephen, a woman who makes mistakes. Miss Rowley's stultifying self-repression is habitual to her; as readers we feel sorry for her but question her stance. In contrast we respond more to Stephen's 'longings and outpourings of heart and soul and mind' (*M* 104) and her bids for freedom. So, when Stephen, in typically New-Womanly fashion, confronts Miss Rowley with the idea that if women want to marry a man they should be allowed to say what they really feel – something which Stephen later does – we realize how far the older woman is weighed down by old-fashioned prejudice and preconceived ideas, ideas which have actually worked to leave her lonely and unfulfilled. Key words used by Stephen here are 'liberty' and 'opportunity', echoing the liberal feminist language of the time. Whilst Miss Rowley, rather like Katey O'Sullivan in *The Primrose Path*, accepts her self-abnegation – and the text implies that she had no choice but to do so – Stephen is an example of the next generation of women who refuse to be 'mute', who advocate sexual relationships based on equality.

The ambiguities in the character of Stephen suggest that Stoker's attitudes to women are more complex – or more confused – than we are sometimes led to expect. Stoker's heroine negotiates and reacts against a set of ideologies that are simultaneously constructs and real for her; her movements are curtailed by them. It is in this sense that the novel can be read as a powerful attack on the subject positions available to Edwardian women. On the other hand, as the story progresses we also get a sense that here, as in other novels, Stoker himself cannot think beyond the restraints of a patriarchal culture and the representations this involves. Something of this is apparent in the way in which Stephen is described physically. In a passage reminiscent of the description of the three female vampires in *Dracula*, the narrator dwells longingly on 'the voluptuous curve of [her] full crimson lips', 'raven eyebrows', 'Eastern blood', the 'something tropical' in her appearance – features which not only suggest that she is 'other' but, according to physiognomic lore, signal the possibility of 'some trouble' which will 'shadow her whole life'. 'Pride, self reliance, dominance and masterdom were all marked in every feature; in her carriage and bearing, and in every twist and turn of her lightest movement.' (*M* 3) The links between female emancipation and distorted sexuality were recurrent ones and it is possible that Stoker's readers would also have read Stephen as an example of the much-feared 'man-woman' who figured in numerous medical treatises of the time, including such ostensibly forward-looking works of sexual science as Richard von Krafft-Ebing's *Psychopathia Sexualis* (1886) and Havelock

Ellis's *Man and Woman* (1894). Some readers may perhaps have recognized in Stoker's description of this 'queer', 'abnormal' girl (*M* 269) some of the language used by Havelock Ellis in his 1886 work 'Sexual Inversion', which led to his pathologization of the robust 'New Woman' into the lesbian. This was a figure characterized by her 'brusque energetic movements...masculine straightforwardness, sense of honour and especially the attitude towards men, free from any suggestion either of shyness or audacity, will often suggest the underlying psychic abnormality to a keen observer.' [24]

One of the main disadvantages faced by Stephen – at least within the logic of the text – is that she, like many of Stoker's heroines, and like many heroines in Victorian fiction more generally, has no mother. In *Dracula*, too, mothers are one of the sources of Lucy Westenra's problems, and it is the containment of what bad mothers represent which the novel moves towards, in its final assertion of motherly virtue in the figure of Mina Harker. In *The Jewel of Seven Stars*, Margaret Trelawny also lacks a mother's protection, and one of the things that makes the ending of *The Primrose Path* so chilling is the realization that Jerry and Katey's children will be motherless and that their prospects are horribly bleak. Stoker stresses again and again throughout his writing career the importance of 'good' (present) mothers, figures whom he identifies with womanliness, health and sexual purity and, in this, he echoes the sentiments of other Victorian and Edwardian ideologues. In *The Man* the male protagonists, Harold and Leonard, are also motherless but in Stephen's case the absence of maternal guidance is shown to have more devastating results, for it results in a troubled young woman forced to try and cope on her own. The narrator makes this clear: 'No one to calm her in the height of her wild abnormal passion! No one to comfort her when the fit had passed! No one to sympathise with her for all that she had suffered! No one to help her build new and better hopes out of the wreck of her mad ideas' (*M* 188). The alarm bells start ringing in a gruesome, almost Gothic, scene in which the adolescent girl discovers her mother's coffin in the crypt of the old church. The discovery makes Stephen hysterical; she faints away in the darkness of the crypt and has to be rescued by Harold. Her first words, after the immediate shock of the encounter are: ' "She was only a girl herself, only just twice my age – lying there in that terrible dark place with all the thick dust and the spiders' webs....How shall I ever bear to think of her lying there and that I shall never see her dear face? Never! Never!" ' (*M* 66) This is clearly a central moment to her in reminding her of what she lacks, but also in formulating a plan of action by which she can avoid a similar fate; the crypt serves (unconsciously perhaps) as a central trope of her vision of women's entrapment within the confined spaces of domesticity.

In contrast, one of the ways in which the text clearly encourages women readers to put up with their sense of discontent is in the prolonged bout of self-castigation which follows Stephen's ill-fated proposal to Leonard Everard, her most outrageous attempt at bucking the conventional values and restrictions of the day:

> 'Leonard', she said softly 'are you sure there is no mistake? Do you not see that I am asking you to be my husband?'
>
> The moment the words were spoken – the bare, hard, naked, shameless words – the revulsion came. As a lightening flash shows up the blackness of the night the appalling truth of what she had done was forced upon her. The blood rushed to her head till cheeks and shoulders and neck seemed to burn. Covering her face with her hands she sank back onto the seat behind her, crying silent bitter tears that seemed to scald her eyes and her cheeks as they ran.
>
> (*M* 136)

Contrary to what Stephen has expected, the proposal is a failure and instead of giving a sense of purpose and closure to her life, leaves her paralyzed by feelings of 'shame' and confusion. As she hurries back to the safety of her bedroom, she is forced to confront what she has done:

> She could not endure herself. Even her own image reflected in her mirror became in a sense loathsome....With an impulse, which did not give her time to think, she blew out her candles and for a little while found relief in the dark....But nothing could shut out the haunting memories of that awful time under the trees on the hilltop....More and more the strain of sensibility was upon her; things present past and future were merely fresh food for horrid thoughts till her brain seemed to be on fire. (*M* 146–8)

This passage is central to the novel because it shows Stephen, defiantly 'Modern' as she may be, defining herself within the dominant middle-class gender categories: angel/whore. Her retreat into self-loathing (a kind of unhealthy, punitive, solitary confinement) and the moment of self-recognition (her sense of her 'self' as a 'fallen' woman) is encoded by the mirror in which she sees her *alter ego*, the demonic 'fallen' woman. As Ann Heilmann has shown, the mirror is, of course, a device often used in fiction as a way of introducing a version of the 'alienated' self or a self split according to existing social conditions, or a deviant self, or a collision with 'sex role' expectations.[25] As we have seen, both *Miss Betty* and *Dracula* deploy this device. Another famous example is the scene in Charlotte Brontë's *Jane Eyre,* where the night before her wedding Jane sees Bertha's reflection (a woman dressed in a bridal veil) in the mirror of her closet. The difference in *The Man* is that the conflict between clashing visions of the self can only be resolved when the heroine rejects one of them. Rescue and the reconstruction of her fragmented self comes from within – by shaking off (in a manner Brontë's governess would undoubtedly have disapproved of) 'all the dross and thought of self' and the discovery of a real (womanly) self where 'nature sweet and simple reigned alone' (*M* 435).

This kind of idealization of the feminine, with its obvious sensitivities to issues of order and tradition, recurs throughout Stoker's texts – spaces which work to reinforce ideas about what is 'normal' showing within the narrative the unhappy consequences of deviating from prescribed codes of conduct. In *The Man* the rules for feminine conduct laid down by society are mocked by Stephen but they are also shown to be vital for the protection of women and the containment of feminine excess, a point made by Miss Rowley for whom the acid test of the here-and-now is what matters. ' "My dear," she tells Stephen, ' "there are many things wrong in our social system. And there are many things, which, though they seem wrong at times, are yet so firmly based on need of human nature that we willingly accept the lesser evil. We women are so constituted that absolute freedom is not possible for us" ' (*M* 92). It is when Stephen ignores these 'facts' by attempting to procure herself a husband that she is most vulnerable and, it is suggested, most dangerous. Whether or not Stoker himself loses his nerve in the last part of the novel is difficult to say, but by its end his heroine has rediscovered the worth of Harold An Wolf, universally acknowledged as a man 'whom to obey would be a natural duty.' (*M* 355) Stephen's choice of Harold as her 'master' is the final awkward, if somewhat predictable, destination of the narrative and one which definitely undermines its standing as the straightforward feminist tract described by contemporary reviewers, for we see a woman who has every chance of enjoying an equal relationship with her husband rejecting any last trace of what the narrator calls her 'militant or even questioning attitude' (*M* 400). Bursting with energetic potential though she may seem, the aspirations of Stephen Norman don't come to very much at all. And, like *Miss Betty* and the short stories in *Dracula's Guest*, the novel characteristically educates its female readers in the problems arising when women try to step outside the separate spheres of action for men and women.

DRACULA'S GUEST

The stories that make up *Dracula's Guest* are so diverse in their subject matter that, like Stoker's novels, it is very difficult to classify them. Introducing the collection in 1914, his widow Florence wrote that they are 'mainly from the earlier period of his strenuous life' and this included the title story, which originated as part of *Dracula* but did not make it to the final version. The stories cover a remarkably wide range of subjects: murder, adultery, degeneration, love, adventure, betrayal; and weird or supernatural events – haunting, the return of the dead, second-sight. Like the novels, they interweave ideas taken from different sources – racial theory, politics, sexology, and psychology. Of the three stories discussed in this chapter, 'The Secret of the Growing Gold' (1892) has an aristocratic setting; 'The Squaw' (1893) is a horrifying account of the death of an American tourist in Nuremberg; 'The Coming of Abel Behenna' (1914) is a regional story set in a small fishing community in rural Cornwall. Given, as we have seen, the penchant for biographical readings of Stoker, some critics have suggested that Stoker's use of the family as an organizing theme in many of these stories and his dramatization of the darker side of male-female relations was prompted by his own experiences as son, husband and employee, or even as a kind of private therapy – a way of tackling his own personal ghosts and sexual hang-ups. Certainly these stories tend to present a very bleak vision of family life; the domestic is a space of safety but also of danger, whose boundaries are shifting and unstable; they focus in uncomfortable ways on the problematics of sexual passion, marriage and on homes in which violence, or the possibility of violence, is always lurking. Behind the smooth façade of home and family, it is suggested, jealousy and passion fester and threaten even the most comfortable of domestic situations. Once again, a key presence is the figure of what Barbara Creed has called the 'monstrous feminine', a figure which can (like many of Stoker's monsters – male or female) be situated in relation to what Julia Kristeva has famously termed 'abjection', namely, that which does 'not respect borders, positions, rules', that which 'disturbs identity, system, order' and which threatens life.[26] In 'The Squaw', the 'savage' malevolent mother of the title is the starting point for interrogating the expected nurturing role of the mother, and the revolution that follows seems to hint that such a role is largely man-made.

An unseasonable short story that Stoker wrote in 1893 for *Holly Leaves* (the Christmas number of the *Illustrated Sporting and Dramatic News*),'The Squaw' is set in Nuremberg, a city which Stoker had visited in 1885. A self-regarding, unnamed Englishman who is touring the region with his new bride, Amelia, narrates it. Also among the party is a boastful, uncouth man from Bleeding Gulch, Nebraska, Elias P. Hutcheson who regales them with stories of his adventures in the American West. Whilst visiting the city's medieval castle, the three tourists climb up to the battlements. Looking down, they see a mother cat on the ground playing with her kitten. Hutcheson drops a pebble down to help the play but misjudges his aim and the stone crushes the kitten's skull. The mother cat glares at Hutcheson, licks the kitten's wound and, realizing that it is dead, tries to climb up the wall looking 'the perfect incarnation of hate.' The angry cat prompts Hutcheson to remember his encounters with the native Indian Apaches and Comanches, in particular, an Indian Squaw who had lingered over the torture of a 'half-breed' who had killed her papoose. The cat stalks Hutcheson, following him and his English companions into the notorious torture tower. Among the gruesome items on display is the infamous 'Iron Virgin', a 'rudely shaped figure of a woman...Mrs Noah in the children's Ark' (DG 59). The tourists learn that in earlier, less civilized times, the prisoner used to be put inside the heavy iron sarcophagus, with the door in front operated by a rope attached to a pulley system. The rust on the inside is due to the blood from the working of the spikes on the inside of the door, which when closed stab the eyes, heart and other organs. The queasy twist to the tale comes when Hutcheson insists on climbing into the contraption ' "jest to see how it feels" ' (DG 61). As the attendant slowly feeds the rope the vengeful mother cat appears. She springs at the attendant who, with blood pouring from his eye and clutching his face in pain, lets go of the rope. Inside, Hutcheson far from enjoying his deadly coupling, is impaled, castrated and his skull crushed. The narrator retrieves the bloody corpse, which the mother cat sits on immediately, licking the blood that 'tricked through the gashed socket of his eyes'. Furious at another man's being unmanned at the hands of the unholy alliance of the iron woman and the cat, the narrator seizes an old executioner's sword and exacts justice against the cat. He '[sheared] her in two as she sat. "No one will call me cruel for doing so" ', he assures us (DG 66). Strikingly we are told that this experience has been so trying to Amelia that her eldest son is born with marks resembling the injuries inflected by the Iron Virgin.

On the surface of it, this bloodthirsty account simply bears out one of the frequent complaints made of Stoker by his contemporaries, namely that his work was unduly violent, that it appealed to readers' animal instincts and included an 'unnecessary number of hideous incidents'.[27] But the charge that 'The Squaw' is merely a blood-fest is undercut when we realize that it is a parable about the rise of American colonial power and the 'white man's burden' (to use Rudyard Kipling's famous phrase), a source of much anxiety in 1890s England. This is one of the intriguing readings suggested by Lillian Nayder in her excellent essay 'Virgin Territory and the Iron Virgin' where she also argues that 'The Squaw' is 'most obviously a story about the settling of the American West...a testimony to the vast energies of the pioneer and a grisly portrait of the antagonism between whites and native Americans in their struggle for the possession of the land', as well as being an exposé of 'the savage behaviour of "civilized" man more generally, in particular the failure of white settlers to distinguish themselves from "savage" Indians in the "wild west"'.[28] According to Nayder, Hutcheson's castration and death in the Iron Virgin brought about by the vengeful mother cat (who, with her blood 'heightened by the blood which still smeared her coat and reddened her mouth', is compared to an Indian Squaw 'covered with her war paint') deliberately 'reminds the reader of the cruel repression involved in the American settler's history.' To take Nayder's argument a step further, we might also argue that this story – which ends littered with corpses – is about a 'past' that can never be forgotten. To quote Eric Sundquist ' "remembrance" is often literally that: one remembers what has been dismembered, reconstructs what has been shattered and atones for what has been ruined or murdered.'[29] In 'The Squaw', Hutcheson's journey is an act of recalling and paying for the costs of America's settlement and colonization.

What is crucial to this story, however, is the very obvious anxiety about powerful women. The female characters in this story fight back. As Nayder has shown, Hutcheson, who clambers into the Iron Virgin ' "jest to see how it feels" ', to have the ' "enjoyment" ' (*DG* 61) represents the colonist-as-rapist, who 'violates virgin territory rather than exploring it' and whose punishment is to be castrated.[30] This can be read as liberating; Hutcheson has got his just desserts. It is, however, another source of the text's anxiety. As Nayder points out, this anxiety is a sexual one: women are aggressors, they 'penetrate and crush' men rather than passively 'receiving them'.[31] However it is not just the Iron Virgin who takes on malevolent qualities. For example, the mother cat is oddly reminiscent of another *fin de siècle* feline presence, namely the one who appears in Sigmund Freud's study of ' "Dora" (*Fragment of An Analysis of a Case of Hysteria*)'. Here, Freud tells his readers that he is completely 'dry and direct' with his patient about sexual matters: 'J'appelle un chat un chat.' However as Jane Gallop has noted:

> At the very moment [Freud] defines non-prurient language as direct and non-euphemistic, he takes a French detour onto a figurative

expression. By his terms, this French sentence would seem to be titillating, coy, and flirtatious. And to make matters juicier (less 'dry'), 'chat' or 'chatte' can be used as vulgar (vulva) slang for the female genitalia. So in this gynaecological context, where he founds his innocence upon the direct use of terms, he takes a French detour and calls a pussy a pussy. [32]

When in 'The Squaw', Stoker feels the need to describe what the story's location in a polite magazine prevents him from saying openly, he, like Freud takes refuge in the coded language of the feline, which in Stoker's case we can assume represents a kind of secret pact between male author and experienced 'men-of-the-world' male readers, those familiar with the sexual slang of their day. It is in this way that we can see connections between the taboo of the 'unsayable' and another displaced but fairly evident worry about rapacious female sexuality, the vagina that kills.

What we also see in this story is that its fears about women's sexuality are also intertwined with a wider anxiety about the figure of the mother, that 'guarantor of identity' who stands at the centre of middle-class ideology as the touchstone of moral and familial virtue.[33] Part of the terror inspired by the Iron Virgin stems from the narrator's sense of her as what Gallop would term a 'phallic mother' who wields the 'phallic tools' of the symbolic order of culture and whose influence must be shaken off.[34] Lillian Nayder has suggested that the Iron Virgin 'is not simply a sexual object; she is a maternal object as well, one compared to Eve and Mrs Noah', from whom the bloodied dismembered Hutcheson is delivered by the narrator in 'a grotesque re-birthing.'[35] We can see this sense of horror as forming part of wider *fin de siècle* discourses on racial health and the role of mothers as good breeders. It is this that lies behind the narrator's treatment of Amelia. As a middle-class mother she is the guardian of legitimacy but she also requires close regulation. It is striking how troubled the text is by the implications of the fact that Amelia does bear the narrator a son and heir but that he has been damaged and disfigured in the process of childbirth. Why is this? Is Amelia really the nervous, delicate (and thus 'normal') woman she seems, who has been traumatized by the events in the castle? Or has she, as Nayder suggests, been inspired by what she has seen, making her own womb 'hostile to patriarchy' – lined with teeth that leave their mark on the chest of male children? Or has the seemingly exemplary Amelia simply been unfaithful and the resultant baby is (uncannily) branded with the marks of his father – Hutcheson – disrupting in another way the narrator's sense of male authority and, by implication, the authority of all Englishmen? Is she like the Iron Virgin then: the narrator's worst nightmare, precisely the kind of autopsying, illegitimating, destabilizing mother that the entire narrative is about trying to keep in her place? The narrator, who tries to foreclose on these violent events and assert his masculine authority leaves the male reader of the *Illustrated Sporting and Dramatic News* to confront the ambivalent distinction between the idealized virtuous mother and the deadly new mother – who may be his own wife.

This story is disturbing partly because it invites us to identify totally with the narrator's point of view and embrace his system of values. The thrust of his ideology seems plain – women's capacity for monstrosity and the need to keep a vigilant watch. Confronted with the story of the Indian Squaw and the slaughter of the mother cat, the narrator remains guiltless and unconcerned. The animalism of his own violence is hidden under the same civilized expressions of disgust, demonstrated by the men who excitedly join in the staking of Lucy Westenra in *Dracula* and Margaret Trelawny in *The Jewel of Seven Stars*, two other young women who are transformed into a version of femininity vile enough to license their extermination by young Englishmen. What Stoker once again hints at is the existence of primal needs and drives in men, which call into question the smooth statements about England as a bastion of civilized values mouthed by the narrator.

Of the stories collected in *Dracula's Guest* in which Stoker exercised his interest in ghosts and hauntings – 'Crooken Sands' (1894), 'The Judge's House' (1891) and 'The Secret of the Growing Gold' (1892) – it is the latter, first glimpsed in the genteel weekly magazine *Black and White*, which could be said to engage most fully at a symbolic level with the issues of gender relations I have been examining in this book. It is also a text that encapsulates in a very stark way the themes of violence and repressed desire, which form the darker subtexts of the stories contained in *Dracula's Guest*. As a ghost story, 'The Secret of the

Growing Gold' is packed full with self-consciously 'uncanny' artefacts and features. It is in one obvious sense a story of decay and imprisonment, haunted like many of Stoker's texts by the traces of influential male writers – Washington Irving, Edgar Allan Poe and Sheridan Le Fanu. It is also a text which may be read as personal; one of the most intriguing aspects of the *Personal Reminiscences* is Stoker's representation of his childhood bedridden self as a powerless gothic hero[ine] – trapped in suffocating interiors, suppressed by the matriarchal restraints embodied in Charlotte Stoker. But 'The Secret of the Growing Gold' is not just about ghosts. Stoker uses the generic conventions of the form of the ghost story to expose female powerlessness and exclusion. He exploits, as many Victorian *female* writers of ghost stories did, the form's potential for exposing the underside of culture. He also draws on its ability to represent what Claire Stewart in a recent essay '"Weird Fascination": The Response to Victorian Women's Ghost Stories', describes as 'women's own marginalization, like the supernatural to the realms of the irrational/Other.'[36] Prior victimization or neglect of women by men or by society more generally provides the explanation for numerous ghost stories by Victorian women writers – as in Margaret Oliphant's 'The Open Door' (1882) or Lucy Clifford's 'Lost' (1883) – stories in which 'the challenge of the supernatural is made directly to notions of masculinity itself'.[37]

'The Secret of the Growing Gold' shows Stoker working in territory that overlaps with these narratives by women. The beautiful Margaret Delandre who has inherited nothing from her family apart from 'the evil tendency of their race...sullen passion, voluptuousness and recklessness' scandalizes her neighbourhood by running off with a neighbour, Geoffrey Brent, 'a handsome wastrel' (*DG* 68–9). Initially, Margaret, who is far from being the downtrodden, self-castigating 'fallen' woman of Victorian stereotype, seems more than capable of taking care of herself. 'Margaret Delandre bore herself so fearlessly and so openly – she accepted her position as the justified companion of Geoffrey Brent so naturally that people came to believe that she was secretly married to him and therefore thought it wiser to hold their tongues lest time should justify her and also make her an active enemy.' (*DG* 70) Several years later, rumours circulate that Margaret has been drowned whilst on a tour of Europe and it seems that, like all those other fallen women of Victorian literature and painting, she has paid the ultimate price for overstepping the mark. In fact she has been murdered – strangled by Geoffrey Brent in order to smooth the way for his marriage to a rich heiress. Geoffrey hastily buries Margaret under the hearthstones in the hall of his ancestral home, unable to move her body without being discovered. In the meantime, Margaret rises from the dead, armed with the power to terrify Brent and his new wife literally to death; they watch in terror as her still-growing hair forces its way through cracks in the broken stones to invade the supposedly-impregnable domestic space.

One of the ways in which Stoker creates his setting and not-so-'secret' motif is by drawing on well-established Gothic conventions and symbolism. As a Gothic story, 'The Secret of the Growing Gold' discloses familiar motifs of confinement, repression, regression and entrapment; the captive woman under threat and the brutish, sexually-threatening, aristocratic man. It also underscores the code in polite society that has moved Geoffrey Brent to violent means to preserve his chance of a good marriage and his reputation, a man for whom life without women and property is unimaginable. There are other Gothic traces. The house, Brent's Rock, for example: '[I]t rose up steeply from the midst of a level region, and for a circuit of a hundred miles it lay on the horizon, with its high old towers and steep roofs cutting the level edge of the wood and hamlet and far scattered mansions' (*DG* 69). Yet whilst the architectural form of the house hints at repression, its Gothic credentials are overturned. Geoffrey Brent begins the story in a position of power but loses it by his act of murdering Margaret, which ensures that their positions get reversed; he succumbs to *her* power to terrorize and destroy him. Brent develops a habit of 'turning suddenly as though someone were speaking from behind him', his newly found pride in home and family is being threatened by the crack in the hearthstone, through which 'were protruding a multitude of threads of golden hair just tinged with grey!', his fear of exposure cohering round what Nickianne Moody, in a discussion of the English ghost story, sees as the most powerful phantom of all: 'a return...of the past'.[38] There are clear parallels here with the ideas played out in 'The Squaw' and *The Jewel of Seven Stars*. Ghosts inevitably and disturbingly represent hidden knowledge so, whilst Margaret Delandre returns with 'distorted features and burning eyes [which] seemed hardly human...', what returns through her is the haunting truth which has been suppressed (*DG* 75).

As a ghost story, 'The Secret of the Growing Gold' has several other important strategies upon which its effects depend. The first is the fact that the haunting arrives not from elsewhere, but instead makes itself felt, as Mark Wigley has written, in an effect of 'surfacing, a return of the repressed as a foreign element that strangely seems to belong to the very domain that renders it foreign'.[39] The second is that whilst the subterranean aspects of the story remind us that Stoker's social landscape is based on the premise of traditional male/female hierarchies, it is the figure of the repressed and excluded sexual woman who becomes empowered. One of the most horrible sensations for Geoffrey Brent is the threat of exposure and imprisonment. Stoker uses Margaret as a device to comment ironically on the male character's sources of security – the ancestral home. By having Brent hurl 'curse after curse on her golden hair' he utilizes a long tradition that associates women's hair with entrapment (*DG* 81). He also uses images of darkness and death to show how women's hair is linked in the masculine imagination with a fear of women's sexuality. To Geoffrey, the hair is something dead but it seems sexually suggestive. To protect his new found respectability and achieve 'closure' on his past life, Geoffrey must kill and bury Margaret, effectively consigning her to a separate and inferior space (literally as well as figuratively, since her corpse is decomposing under the floor).

Barbara Belford, in her biography of Stoker, suggests that the starting point for 'The Secret of the Growing Gold' was a piece of high-society gossip involving an actual figure. One night in 1869, at Highgate Cemetery, the pre-Raphaelite poet and painter, Dante Gabriel Rossetti, exhumed his wife, Elizabeth Siddall, seven years after her death. Rossetti, who was by this time experiencing his own sense of (psychic) decomposition, intended to retrieve a notebook containing copies of his unpublished poems. When the coffin was opened, the poems were retrieved from the strands of Siddall's still-growing blonde hair. Stoker was sufficiently intrigued by the events to record it. However, 'The Secret of the Growing Gold' is not only of interest because of its origins in a contemporary scandal. It can also fruitfully be read as a *fin de siècle* social document. Its deployment of the matrix of degeneration suggests that the history of the Brent family is tied up with the widespread sense of high society's decadence in the 1890s. Some readers might have noted the way in which the tenor of Stoker's language seems to be inspired by such texts as T. H. Huxley's famous lecture 'Evolution and Ethics' (1893), which addressed the widespread sense of ennui and the 'over stimulation' and 'exhaustion' of modern civilization.[40] Geoffrey Brent is a familiar Stoker type, the effete aristocrat, the vampire, the absentee landlord, an unequivocal brute who is irredeemably degenerate: 'a type of worn out race' (*DG* 69) whose existence is underpinned by a long history of exploitation. He begins the story as the sole representative of the family and he takes a pride in being the only inheritor, the last custodian of its corrupt values. The narrator likens him to one of 'those antique Italian nobles whom the painters have preserved to us with their courage, the unscrupulousness, their refinement of lust and cruelty – the voluptuary actual with the fiend potential' (*DG* 69). In this way, the gremlins of other texts and stories – of which literary gossip is only the most persistent or obvious – haunt the very structure of the story. Geoffrey Brent is also reminiscent of Oscar Wilde's Dorian Gray – a selfish man who is forced finally to realize the horror of his own moral decay – and of Rochester in *Jane Eyre*, another man who entombs an inconvenient female.

There is one other feature of note here and that is the presence of the new Mrs Brent, a wealthy but child-like woman who relies on her degenerate husband to order her world. On one level, she seems cast in the Jane Eyre mould, brought to a house in which there is a previous vengeful wife still lurking. However, unlike Brontë's heroine, her role is very passive. Her main failing is her inattention to her husband's moral obliquity. She lives her life based on what is unknown, unseen, unarticulated: Mrs Brent (she has no other name) has accepted the status quo of sexual double standards. In this sense her marriage exemplifies something of the middle and upper-class Victorian marriage where respectability is upheld by not talking about certain 'nasty' subjects. In effect, she collaborates in her own oppression, willing to be confined (she is also pregnant) in the interests of her unscrupulous husband. Yet as we have seen, marriage was a social institution undergoing transition at this time and what happens in 'The Secret of the Growing Gold' is that the growing hair creeping out from the floor represents the knowledge of the husband's hidden life, which can no longer be ignored. As Brent, angry with his wife, lets out a string of obscenities, he suddenly stops as he sees 'a new look of terror in his wife's eyes. He followed her glance, and then he too, shuddered – for there on the broken hearth-stone, lay a golden streak as the point of the hair rose through the crackle ' "Look, look!" she shrieked. "Is it some ghost of the past!" ' (DG 81) As Mrs Brent finally begins to understand the significance of what she sees and awakes to the Gothic horrors that surround her, she falls into 'a raging fever', her nervous sensibility unable to stand the shock.

This power of the past to haunt the present is also behind the impact of the final text under discussion here. 'The Coming of Abel Behenna' is a story which also returns to the themes of male possessiveness and male bonding already marked out in Stoker's full-length novels. Like several of the stories which make up the twists and turns of *Dracula's Guest*, it is also about the way in which the 'abject' can be experienced, particularly in relation to sexual and erotic desire. Stoker also invokes the popular plot device of the fatal return, a narrative which, as several critics have noted, had a special resonance for Victorian readers given that this was an age of expansionist foreign policies and increasing emigration, with men seeking to make their fortunes in distant lands before returning home, rich and prosperous.[41] One thinks of Emily Brontë's *Wuthering Heights* (1848), Elizabeth Gaskell's *Sylvia's Lovers* (1860), Mary Braddon's *Lady Audley's Secret* (1862) and Alfred Tennyson's poem 'Enoch Arden' (1864), about the return from overseas of a man believed dead who discovers that his wife has remarried. Stoker repeats these ideas but typically takes them a stage further towards a horrible conclusion. Most of the action takes place in Pencastle, a small Edenic fishing port in Cornwall. The monstrous appetite for men, blood and money, demonstrated by Lucy Westenra in *Dracula* or Arabella March in *The Lair of the White Worm*, is not quite so blatantly in evidence here but the narrative is driven by the demands made by the heroine, Sarah Trefusis, and her greedy mother that (as a married woman) Sarah be provided with a comfortable lifestyle by one of her suitors: Eric Sansom or Abel Behenna. Whilst remembering her relationship with Abel, who having staked his claim to Sarah by the lucky toss of a coin, dutifully sails off to China and the East Indies in order to satisfy her hunger for money, Sarah, with 'woman's weaker nature', consoles herself with Eric (*DG* 107). For his own selfish motives, Eric persuades Sarah that Abel is dead. Having satisfied herself that she can access the money freshly deposited in Abel's bank account, Sarah agrees to replace Abel with Eric. Two weeks before the wedding there is a violent storm and a ship is wrecked in the harbour. Climbing aboard to help rescue the crew, Eric comes face to face with one of them – Abel:

> On the instant, a wave of passion swept through Eric's heart. All his hopes were shattered, and with the hatred of Cain his eyes looked out. He saw in the instant of recognition the joy in Abel's face that his was the hand to succour him, and this intensified his hate. Whilst the passion was on him he started back, and the rope ran out between his hands. His moment of hate was followed by an impulse of his better manhood, but it was too late.
>
> Before he could recover himself, Abel encumbered with the rope that should have aided him, was plunged with a despairing cry back into the darkness of the devouring sea. (*DG* 113)

There is no sense of brotherhood on Eric's part here; only naked self-interest. His associations with savagery and the suggestion that his behaviour is not that of 'manhood' but a throwback to some former, less civilized era, contrasts with Abel's helplessness. However, even when apparently out of the picture, Abel has the power to disrupt events and he does so on Eric and Sarah's wedding day (on what is actually supposed to be Abel and Sarah's wedding day). He comes back from the most frightening destination of all – death – to demand recognition of his rights – to Sarah, to his money, and the domesticity he has been promised:

> When the bridal couple had passed through...the remainder of the congregation...were startled by a long shrill scream from the bride. They rushed through the passage and found her on the bank with wild eyes pointing to the river bed opposite Eric Sanson's door. The

falling tide had deposited there the body of Abel Behenna stark upon the broken rocks. The rope trailing from its waist had been twisted from the current round the mooring post, and had held it back whilst the tide had ebbed away from it. The right elbow had fallen in a chink in the rock, leaving the hand outstretched toward Sarah, with the open palm upward as though it were extended to receive hers, the pale drooping fingers open to the clasp. (*DG* 199)

This tableau is a neat touch. It carries greater impact than any exchange of dialogue or any intrusive narrative explanation. The outstretched hand is a signal that Eric and Sarah are incomplete - sterile, impotent, ultimately doomed – without Abel. Their marriage is cursed.

Even though it looks back to earlier literary models, 'The Coming of Abel Behenna' clearly signals its intention that this is a modern story about self-interest and self-preservation. Stoker, we should remember, grew up in a post-Darwinian age. The publication of *The Origin of Species* in 1859 had helped expose a world of violence, fighting and suffering, in which the strongest to survive were not necessarily the noblest. Abel's return from the dead – and his biting back, as it were – can be read as a bleak comment on the failure of romantic love in a world full of competing individual appetites and ambitions. The story can also be read as a narrative about exclusion. Removed from Sarah, separated from her and from Pencastle, Abel becomes a creature of margin as well as burden. Once out of sight, he is also out of mind and once Sarah has agreed to marry Eric, he can only return as a troubling ghost. Reading the story in the wider context of 1890s imperialism (with which Stoker's readers would have been familiar) there are grounds for suggesting that, like *Dracula,* this is also a cautionary story about imperial as well as domestic exploitation: Abel becomes part of the Empire, spending his days in foreign lands and sending his hard-earned money back home. When he does finally return, Dracula-like, an unexpected and unwelcome visitor glimpsed by terrified witnesses, he is represented in terms which emphasize his foreignness or his 'Otherness': 'a strange seaman whom no one knew'; a 'porpoise', a weird creature ' "like a pig with the entrails out" ' (*DG* 117–18); he is no longer the handsome young man Sarah remembers but a less than human being who exists only to support the English home. Abel is completely marginalized and dispossessed; his place usurped by the blond Aryan Eric and the domestic sphere redrawn to exclude the outsider.[42]

Critics interested in issues of gender might also say that what makes this story especially interesting is the use it makes of the triangle configuration, so common to Victorian fiction, of one woman loved by two men; the woman marries the losing suitor after the first has disappeared. The effects of this erotic triangle are present everywhere in Stoker's work, in both fiction and non-fiction: Stoker's biographers have made much of Stoker competing with Oscar Wilde for the attentions of Florence Balcombe. Stoker, as we know, was the victor. In 'The Coming of Abel Behenna' Stoker sets up a simple contrast between the two male characters, the fair haired 'Norseman' Eric Sansom and the dark 'gypsy' Abel Behenna and, in doing so, writes out an example of that homosocial desire described by Eve Sedgwick in *Between Men* centring on a type of male bonding that is often violently homophobic, based on the exchange of women, and yet is closely linked to homosexuality.[43] Both men are presented as paragons of masculinity, robust, vigorous, straightforward, who 'seemed to have singled out each other from the very beginning to work and strive together, to fight each other and to stand back to back in all endeavours' (*DG* 98) but their masculine friendship, which Stoker likens to that of Damon and Pythias and describes as a 'Temple of Unity', is destroyed because of their rivalry over Sarah Trefusis. As a female character in a short story about male friendship written by a man, the function of Sarah seems fairly predictable; by captivating both men, this sadistic character allows Stoker once again to associate the figure of 'woman' with death and destruction and moral emptiness. She is a life-denying rather than life-giving force. '[H]er one intention...was so to arrange matters that [she]... should get all that was possible out of both men.'''"Both these men want ye"', her mother tells her, '"and only one can have ye, but before ye chose it'll be so arranged that ye'll have all that both have got"' (*DG* 100).

In this sense 'The Coming of Abel Behenna' is a thoroughly misogynistic text in its analysis of male-female relations. From a different perspective, however, it may also be that what Stoker wanted to emphasize were the kinds of negotiations any young woman might find herself caught up in on her way to satisfying

society's expectations. Whilst the text portrays Sarah's behaviour as shabby and amoral, it is also possible to read her as a
victim of sorts – in this instance of the homosocial world of her
community. Sarah is, like the heroines of *The Fate of Fenella, Miss
Betty* and *The Man*, depicted as on her own, without proper
guidance, in a male-dominated environment. The young men
who surround Sarah, 'boiling with jealousy', regard her merely
as a trophy to be fought over and the text implies that Sarah's
existence, like that of all other women, cannot be separated from
the self-absorption of the men who lay claim to her.

The sense of disturbance in 'The Coming of Abel Behenna',
like the other stories in *Dracula's Guest* discussed here, invites
inspection by anyone interested in studying the issues
surrounding the topic of 'male feminist voices'. Stoker's
attempts to survey the choices and restrictions imposed on
women leads him to numerous representations of – and
reflections on – patriarchy, whilst his own performance leads
him to adopt many voices. But in trying to locate Stoker's
writings about women within some of the contexts in which
they were produced and read, we have seen that the situation is
complex. All of Stoker's texts stress the 'natural' differences
between the sexes and 'woman's nature' (*D* 235). They also
counsel – as in another late novel, *Lady Athlyne* (1908) – the need
for the female reader to remember that she is after all 'more
primitive than man', that '[h]er instincts are more self-centred
than his', that her life is destined to 'move...in a narrower circle'
(*LA* 154). His novels also validate female intelligence and
initiative, and question the sexual double standard. They suggest
that female fulfilment and a sense of self is desirable. Thus in
The Man, for example, Stephen Norman is represented losing
her moral bearings but also as trapped in that part of the new
twentieth century, still governed by Victorian assumptions and
she retains the readers' sympathies throughout. Indeed, sympathy for Stephen's social and moral confusion, her intelligence,
her resourcefulness, and her feelings of imprisonment increase
the more she sublimates herself within approved kinds of
behaviour and does so in a rather confused and cheerless way.

Yet the fate of all the heroines discussed in this chapter, in
particular Betty Pole and Fenella Ffrench, also suggests that
women can only really be safe and fulfilled within a conven-

tional family unit as loving wives and mothers. Unruly, transgressive, excessive female figures tend to be chastened – either by marriage or violent death. Thus exactly how we are meant to read these rebellious women who re-appear through-out Stoker's work remains a point of debate. Do we cheer when they are vanquished? Or do these monstrously energetic women represent fantasies of escape from gender roles? Nancy K. Miller has argued, of women-centred fiction, that those texts that fall short of verisimilitude and depend on unrealistic narrative turns 'manifest an extravagant wish for the story to turn out differently.'[44] That is, they suggest rebellion against the restraints of the respectable plot. Certainly it is true that whilst the endings of Stoker's narratives have a tendency to close up the gaps within contemporary ideologies of gender and re-establish 'normality', they clearly do reveal the cracks within these systems. As we saw in the previous chapter on Stoker's adventure fiction, one of our tasks as readers is to be alert to these seeming contradictions and to decide whether Stoker himself offers an endorsement or critique of his society's values.

Conclusion

This book has sought to trace some of the issues of identity, gender and race through a sample of Stoker's texts written at different stages in his career. As I have suggested, Stoker is in many ways a wide-ranging writer, of more complexity than he has been credited for; a writer who was responsive to the social concerns of his day and to the expanding market for fiction that emerged in the 1890s and 1900s. This points us toward Stoker's status as a very accommodating writer whose texts can be approached through many frameworks.

The emphasis placed on Stoker as a writer who experimented with different fictional sub-genres – the historical romance, the adventure story, the temperance novel, the ghost story, the Gothic novel and the 'New Woman' novel – is an indicator of his sense of himself as a commercial writer. It also reminds us that it is insufficient to accept the rigidity with which forms like the vampire or horror novel have been applied as containers for his work and which, for the most part, have been used to find the rest of his fictions less interesting than those of his contemporaries. It is true that the bulk of the critical attention which Stoker has received is still directed at *Dracula* but the evidence of contemporary reviews reminds us that Stoker's original readers and reviewers found it rather more difficult to contain him in a single category or via single work. Other novels and stories merit attention, not only as examples of popular fiction but as cultural documents that engage late-Victorian and Edwardian ideas on identity, gender, race, morality and the family.

Stoker was not a literary rebel and the critics of the day and his bourgeois readers generally found his fiction acceptable (though there were exceptions, as we have seen). Nonetheless, one of the aims of this short book has been to suggest that

Stoker's novels are less simplistic and more challenging than they might at first appear. That this is so in the case of *Dracula* is of course a critical commonplace. Yet this study has also attempted to raise questions about the engagement and ideological content of Stoker's fiction more generally. This way of reading Stoker's works, as texts that engage with important nineteenth and early twentieth-century political and cultural ideas, has been one of the most positive developments in recent criticism. There is a growing acceptance that the Stoker as revealed in his novels is not so much the 'childish' (Laurence Irving's description) theatrical hanger-on but a knowledgeable and well-read figure, part of a dynamic network of prominent writers, politicians and artists. The relationships to Stoker's work of the political and social theories of such famous figures as Havelock Ellis, William Gladstone, H.M. Stanley, Walt Whitman, and Oscar Wilde, to say nothing of the 'New Woman' and the New Imperialism, are beginning to be established.

Yet to return Stoker to his rightful place in literary history is not to stabilize him. He remains inherently contradictory. Like a holograph he seems to shift. He is at once devoted son, Irish outsider, loyal servant, the hearty epitome of English muscular Christianity, sexual neurotic, scandalous master of horror fiction, and harbinger of the commercial degradation of fiction. Although he may seem to refuse to fit neatly into any of the patterns of feminist or postcolonial historiography, it is difficult to dispute that he confounds some of the expectations about men of his time. His work had wider appeal than he has been given credit for and, although he is now condemned as conservative, one of the attractions of his writing is its polyphony, and thus its potential to resist fixed readings. Stoker's novels, which struck a chord with many Victorian and Edwardian readers, are worthy of rescue and revaluation. The trademark name 'Bram Stoker' may not be interchangeable with 'Oscar Wilde', 'Robert Louis Stevenson' or 'Henry James' but they are all part of the same cultural scene that we will perceive only in a distorted way, as long as the bulk of Stoker's work continues to be ignored. But while the critical rehabilitation of these more famous contemporaries continues, that of Stoker is long overdue and is only just getting underway.

Notes

INTRODUCTION

1 'Bram Stoker', *The Times*, 22 April 1912, 15.
2 Hall Caine, 'Bram Stoker: The Story of a Great Friendship', *Daily Telegraph*, 24 April 1912, 16.
3 See *The Dracula Society* (http://www.thedraculasociety.org.uk/) and *Dracula's Castle* (http://www.draculascastle.com/).
4 See Ronald Thomas, 'Specters of the Novel: *Dracula* and the Cinematic Afterlife of the Victorian Novel', *Nineteenth-Century Contexts*, 22: 1 (2000), 77–102.
5 Philip Howard, 'Tory Fortunes May Be Rocky But They Do A Good Horror Show', *The Times*, 16 May 1997, 22.
6 Newspaper articles reporting Michael Howard's bid to become Leader of the Conservative Party in October 2003 continued this theme. James Hardy's report in *The Mirror* was headlined 'Dracula Stakes His Claim' and continued: 'Michael Howard was in the shadows waiting to grab the Tory Leadership last night after MPs sank their fangs into Iain Duncan Smith'. This article (which also wrote that Howard's parents were Transylvanian) was accompanied by a mocked-up photo of Michael Howard wearing an opera coat and fangs. *Daily Mirror*, 30 October 2003, 1.
7 Kim Newman, 'Fangs Ain't What They Used To Be', *The Independent*, 14 June 1997, 18.
8 Paul Wilkinson, 'Dracula Fans Loose Stake in Cemetery', *The Times*, 10 February 1997, 8.
9 Roger Boyes, 'Romanian Military Gives Dracula a Whirl', *The Times*, 24 May 1997, 16.
10 Ian Chadband, 'Waugh's Count Draculas Bloodied but Unbeatable', *Evening Standard* 25 June 2001, 67.
11 For a brief discussion of the influence of Stoker on late-twentieth-century novelists see Margaret Carter, 'Revampings of Dracula in Contemporary Fiction', *Journal of Dracula Studies*, 3 (2001), 10–15.

12 Caryn James 'Happy Birthday, Undead', *New York Times*, 13 March 1997, 46.

13 Helen Carter, 'Vampire Killer Must Serve Twelve Years', *The Guardian*, 3 August 2002, 3.

14 Jonathan Jones, 'Running Back to Mummy', *The Guardian*, 27 June 1998, 4.

15 Carol Margaret Davison (ed.), *Bram Stoker's Dracula: Sucking Through the Century, 1897–1997* (Toronto: University of Toronto Press, 1997), 30.

16 Eric Korn, 'The Devil's Own Job', *Times Literary Supplement*, 17 November 1995, 8.

17 More recently, in an *Observer* exposé, Stephen Khan reports that 'Vampirism' is a rapidly growing youth cult and its followers are increasing in number – and they take *Dracula* as their handbook. Stephen Khan, 'Real-life Evil Lurking Behind the Vampire Cult', *The Observer*, 26 October 2003.

18 Nina Auerbach, *Our Vampires, Ourselves* (Chicago: University of Chicago Press, 1995), 35.

19 Ibid.

20 Ed Power, 'An Irishman's Diary', *Irish Times*, 3 June 2000, 24.

21 Francis Ford Coppola, 'Introduction', *Bram Stoker's 'Dracula': The Film and The Legend* (New York: Newmarket Press, 1992), ii.

22 [Unsigned Article], 'Bram Stoker', *New York Times*, 23 April 1912, 12.

23 [Unsigned Article], 'Bram Stoker', *British Weekly*, 25 April 1912, 74.

24 Bram Stoker to Walt Whitman, 18 February 1872, cited in Barbara Belford, *Bram Stoker: A Biography of the Author of Dracula* (London: Weidenfeld & Nicolson, 1996), 42–3.

25 Cited in Harry Ludlam, *A Biography of Dracula: The Life Story of Bram Stoker* (London: Foulsham, 1962), 67.

26 Hall Caine, *My Story* (London: Heinemann, 1908), 349.

27 William Hughes and Andrew Smith (eds.), *Bram Stoker: History, Psychoanalysis and the Gothic* (London: Macmillan, 1998), 6.

28 Details of recent biographical work are given in the Bibliography.

29 Tony Bennett, 'The Politics of "the Popular" and Popular Culture', in Tony Bennett, Colin Mercer, and Janet Wollacott (eds.), *Popular Culture and Social Relations* (Milton Keynes: Open University, 1986), 19.

30 David Glover, *Vampires, Mummies and Liberals: Bram Stoker and the Politics of Popular Fiction* (London: Duke University Press, 1996), 4.

31 Fredric Jameson, *The Political Unconscious: Narrative as a Socially Symbolic Act* (London: Methuen, 1981), 141. See also John Cawelti, *Adventure, Mystery and Romance: Formula Stories as Art and Popular Culture* (Chicago: Chicago University Press, 1976); Franco Moretti, *Signs Taken for Wonders: Essays in the Sociology of Literary Forms* (London: Verso, 1983).

CHAPTER 1: STOKER AND THE CRITICS

1 [Unsigned Review], *'The Watter's Mou'*, *Yorkshire Post*, 3 January 1895, 3.

2 [Unsigned Review], *'The Watter's Mou'*, *St. James' Gazette*, 12 February 1895, 5–6; [Unsigned Review], *'The Watter's Mou'*, *The Speaker*, 9 February 1895, 166; [Unsigned Review], 'The Trail of the Vampire', *St. James' Gazette*, 30 June 1897, 5.

3 [Unsigned Review], *'The Shoulder of Shasta'*, *The Spectator*, 22 February 1896, 273.

4 [Unsigned Article], 'A Chat about Books', *Daily Mail*, 6 August 1897, 3.

5 Cited in Belford, *Bram Stoker*, 312.

6 This is also the impression given in Horace Wyndham, *The Nineteen Hundreds* (New York: Thomas Seltzer, 1923). 'To see Stoker in his element was to see him standing at the top of the theatre's stairs, surveying a "first-night" crowd trooping up them. There was no mistake about it, a Lyceum premiere did draw an audience that really was representative of the best of that period in the realms of art, literature and society. Admittance was a very jealously guarded privilege. Stoker, indeed, looked upon the stalls, dress circle and boxes as if they were annexes to the Royal Enclosure at Ascot and one almost had to be proposed and seconded before the coveted ticket would be issued' (119).

7 Philip Amory 'Mr and Mrs John Bull Pretend', *The Comet: A Magazine of Free Opinion*, May 1897, 30.

8 Bram Stoker, 'The Censorship of Fiction', *The Nineteenth Century and After*, 64, September 1908, 481.

9 [Unsigned Article], 'Sir Henry Irving', *Blackwood's Magazine*, 180, (1906) 621.

10 Laurence Irving, *Henry Irving: The Actor and his World* (London: Faber, 1951), 174, 294, 453.

11 [Unsigned Article], 'Sir Henry Irving', *Blackwood's Magazine*, 180, (1906) 621.

12 Hall Caine, 'Bram Stoker: The Story of a Great Friendship', *Daily Telegraph*, 24 April 1912, 16.

13 Hans Robert Jauss, *Toward an Aesthetic of Reception* (Minnesota: University of Minnesota Press, 1982), 27.

14 Cherry A Hankin (ed.), *Letters Between Katherine Mansfield and John Middleton Murray* (London: Virago, 1988), 204.

15 [Unsigned Article], 'Bram Stoker', *Daily Telegraph*, 23 April 1912, 6.

16 H.P. Lovecraft, *Supernatural Horror in Literature* (New York: Ben Abramsom, 1945), 78.

17 [Unsigned Article], 'Mr Bram Stoker', *Irish Times*, 24 April 1912, 9.

18 Unlike Oscar Wilde, Stoker receives no mention in W. J. McCormack's *Ascendancy and Tradition in Anglo-Irish Literary History from 1789–1939* (1985). Two recent books Seamus Deane's *Strange Country: Modernity and Nationhood in Irish Writing since 1790* (1997) and Joseph Valente's *Dracula's Crypt: Bram Stoker, Irishness and the Question of Blood* (2002) have finally suggested that Stoker's Irish background is deserving of serious attention.

19 See *The Wasteland*, Section V, 'What the Thunder Said', l. 380. I am grateful to Stephen Arata for drawing my attention to this reference.

20 Maurice Richardson, 'The Psychoanalysis of Ghost Stories', *Twentieth Century*, 166, (1959), 427.

21 Ludlam, *A Biography of Dracula*, 107.

22 Details of these are given in the bibliography.

23 Carol Senf, '*Dracula*: Stoker's Response to the New Woman', *Victorian Studies*, 26 (1982), 33–49.

24 John Sutherland, *The Longman Companion to Victorian Fiction* (London: Longman, 1988), 1.

25 See Peter D. Macdonald, *British Literary Culture and Publishing Practice 1880–1914* (Cambridge: Cambridge University Press, 1997).

26 William Hughes, *Beyond Dracula: Bram Stoker's Fiction and its Cultural Contexts*, (London: Macmillan, 2000), 177.

27 Glover, *Vampires, Mummies and Liberals*, 23.

28 Daniel Farson, *The Man Who Wrote Dracula* (London: Joseph, 1975), 207. Farson also read *The Lair of The White Worm* as another very personal novel in which the reader can detect the disintegrating relations between Stoker and his wife: 'Bram's guilt at rejecting Florence can be found seeping through its pages' (224, 216).

29 Margot Peters, 'The Boss From Hell', *New York Times*, 7 April 1996, 78.

30 Malcolm Sutcliffe, *Dracula Revealed Style, Theme, Archetype and Echoes of Bram Stoker* (London: Sutcliffe, 1999), 213.

31 [Unsigned Review], '*The Mystery of the Sea*', *Punch*, 123 (20 August 1902), 110.

32 [Unsigned Article], 'Sir Henry Irving', *Blackwood's Magazine*, 180, (1906) 621.

33 C. F. Moberley Bell to Bram Stoker, 28 May 1897, Stoker Collection, Brotherton Library, University of Leeds.

34 Talia Schaffer, ' "A Wilde Desire Took me": The Homoerotic History of Dracula', *ELH* 61:2 (1994), 381–426.

35 Ed Cohen, 'The Double Lives of Man: Narration and Identification in Late Nineteenth-Century Representations of Ec-Centric Masculinities', in Sally Ledger and Scott McCracken (eds.), *Cultural Politics at the Fin de Siècle* (Cambridge: Cambridge University Press, 1995), 85–114.

36 Byrne R. S. Fone, *A Road to Stonewall: Male Homosexuality and Homophobia in English and American Literature 1750–1969* (New York: Twayne, 1995).

37 Ibid.

38 Howard Malchow, in *Gothic Images of Race in Nineteenth Century Britain* (Stanford: Stanford University Press, 1996), argues that the adult Stoker projects in his novels an idealized self-image of himself, as part of a 'determinedly unsexual homosexual' group. He argues that it is Stoker's 'need to portray this – to himself as well as to others – in terms that do not suggest the effeminate male and to avoid being "misjudged", which results in the blurring of gender boundaries in *Dracula* and indeed other works' (146).

39 Joseph Bierman, 'A Critical Stage in the Writing of *Dracula*', in William Hughes and Andrew Smith (eds.), *Bram Stoker, History, Psychoanalysis and the Gothic* (London: Palgrave, 1998), 151, 167.

40 'The Shadow Builder', cited in Bierman, 'A Critical Stage', 165.

41 Jeffrey Richards, 'Gender, Race and Sexuality in Bram Stoker's Other Novels', in Christopher Parker (ed.), *Gender Roles and Sexuality in Victorian Literature* (Aldershot: Scolar Press, 1995), 143.

42 Glover, *Vampires, Mummies and Liberals*, 4.

43 Cited in Rob Dixon, *Writing the Colonial Adventure* (Cambridge: Cambridge University Press, 1995), 3.

44 Ibid.

45 Max Nordau, *Degeneration* (London: William Heinemann, 1975), 7–8.

46 Malchow, *Gothic Images of Race*, 4.

47 Richards, 'Gender, Race and Sexuality', 170.

48 Mrs Boyd Carpenter to Bram Stoker, 11 July 1897, in Glover, *Vampires, Mummies and Liberals*, 4.

49 [Unsigned Review], 'Miss Betty', *North British Daily Review*, 28 February 1898, 2.

50 Robert Scholes, *Textual Power: Literary Theory and the Teaching of English* (London: Yale University Press, 1985), 33.

51 See: John Brannigan, 'Power and Its Representation', in Julian Wolfreys and William Baker (eds.), *Literary Theories* (London: Macmillan, 1996), 157–76.

52 Laura Marholm, 'Neurotic Keynotes' (1896), in Angelique Richardson (ed.), *Women Who Did* (London: Penguin, 2002), xlix.

53 Maud Churton Braby, *Modern Marriage and How to Bear It*, in Sandra Kemp, Charlotte Mitchell and David Trotter, *Edwardian Fiction: An Oxford Companion* (Oxford: Oxford University Press, 1997), xiv.

54 Kate Millett, *Sexual Politics* (New York: Doubleday, 1970).

55 Toril Moi, *Sexual Textual Politics: Feminist Literary Theory* (London: Methuen, 1985), 65

56 Ibid, 58.

57 Michael Ryan, *Literary Theory* (Oxford: Blackwell, 1999), 105.
58 Ruth Robbins, *Literary Feminisms* (Basingstoke: Macmillan, 2000), 109.
59 Laura Claridge and Elisabeth Langland (eds.), *Out of Bounds: Male Writers and Gender* (Massachusetts: Massachusetts University Press, 1990), x.

CHAPTER 2: LONDON IN VIEW

1 Joseph Valente, *Dracula's Crypt: Bram Stoker, Irishness and the Question of Blood* (Urbana: University of Illinois Press, 2002), 33.
2 Henry James, 'Miss Braddon', *Nation,* 9 November 1865, 594.
3 Glennis Byron, 'Introduction', *Dracula* (Peterborough: Broadview Press, 1998), 15.
4 Henry James, *The Princess Casamassima* (London: Penguin, 1987), 34–5.
5 'Lorna', 'Mr Bram Stoker: A Chat with the Author of Dracula', *British Weekly*, 1 July 1897, 185.
6 Glover, *Vampires, Mummies and Liberals*, 26.
7 Cited in Glover, *Vampires, Mummies and Liberals*, 72.
8 See Chris Baldick and Robert Mighall, 'Gothic Criticism' in David Punter (ed.), *A Companion to the Gothic* (Oxford: Blackwell, 2000), 209–28. Baldick and Mighall object to the critical predisposition to describe *fin de siècle* culture as anxiety-ridden, and Stoker's text as subversive. This stems, they suggest, from the tendency of modern critics to re-affirm their own values in discussions of *Dracula*.
9 See Lyn Pykett, 'Sensation and the Fantastic in the Victorian Novel' in Deirdre David (ed.), *The Cambridge Companion to the Victorian Novel* (Cambridge: Cambridge University Press, 2001), 192–211.
10 Glover, *Vampires, Mummies and Liberals*, 93.
11 Ibid, 29.
12 See Kathleen McCormack, 'Intoxication and the Victorian Novel', in William Baker and Kenneth Womack (eds.), *A Companion to the Victorian Novel* (London: Greenwood Press, 2002), 137–150.
13 Ibid.
14 Judith Halberstam, *Skin Shows: Gothic Horror and the Technology of Monsters* (Durham: Duke University Press, 1995), 72.
15 For an extended discussion of this trope see: Gretchen Murphy, 'Enslaved Bodies: Figurative Slavery in the Temperance Fiction of Harriet Beecher Stowe and Walt Whitman', *Genre,* 28 (1995), 100.
16 This reading has been prompted by a useful introduction to Marxist approaches to literary texts i.e. Jessica Maynard's, ' "Snowed Up": Marxist Approaches', in Julian Wolfreys and William Baker (eds.), *Literary Theories* (London: Macmillan, 1996), 130.
17 Cited in David Glover, *Vampires, Mummies and Liberals*, 68.

18 P. J. Keating, *Into Unknown England 1866–1913: Selections from the Social Explorers* (Manchester: Manchester University Press, 1979), 546.

19 See Murphy, 'Enslaved Bodies, 100, for an extended discussion of this idea.

20 Ibid.

21 Leonore Davidoff and Catherine Hall, *Family Fortunes: Men and Women of the English Middle-Class, 1780–1850* (Cambridge: Cambridge University Press, 1987), 108–9; 114–15.

22 John Ruskin, 'Of Queen's Gardens', *Sesame and Lillies* (1865; London: George Allen, 1901), 107–9.

23 Lydia Sigourney, *Water Drops* (New York, 1850), v. In Karen Sanchez-Eppler, 'Temperance in the Bed of a Child', in David S. Reynolds and Debra J. Rosenthal (eds.), *The Serpent in the Cup. Temperance in American Literature* (Amhurst: University of Massachusetts Press, 1997), 62. See also Murphy, 'Enslaved Bodies', 104–5.

24 John Ruskin, 'Of Queen's Gardens', 73.

25 Frances Power Cobbe, 'Wife Torture in England', *The Contemporary Review*, 32 (1878), 55–87, in Monika Rydygier Smith, 'Trollope's Dark Vision', *Victorian Review* 22 (1986), 21.

26 J. S. Mill, *The Subjection of Women* (1869: New York: Dover, 1997), 34–5.

27 Bram Dijkstra, *Idols of Perversity: Fantasies of Femininity in Fin de Siècle Culture* (New York: Oxford University Press, 1986), 345. For a recent analysis of the 'bloofer lady' episode see Leslie Ann Minot, 'Vamping the Children: The "Bloofer Lady", the London Minotaur and Child Victimization in late-Nineteenth Century England', in Andrew Maunder and Grace Moore (eds.), *Victorian Crime, Madness and Sensation* (Aldershot: Ashgate, 2004), 228–42.

28 [Unsigned Review], *'Dracula', Glasgow Herald,* 10 June 1897, 10.

29 [Unsigned Review], *'Dracula,' Daily News,* 27 May 1897, 6.

30 [Unsigned Article], 'The Trail of the Vampire', *St. James' Gazette*, 30 June 1897, 5.

31 Florence Marryat, *Blood of the Vampire* (London: Hutchinson, 1897), 121. See Sian Macfie 'They Suck Us Dry: A Study of Late Nineteenth Century Projections of Vampiric Women', in Philip Shaw and Peter Stockwell (eds.), *Subjectivity and Literature from the Romantics to the Present Day* (London: Pinter, 1991), 58–67.

32 Mary Braddon to Bram Stoker, 23 June 1897, Stoker Collection, Brotherton Library, University of Leeds.

33 Belford, *Bram Stoker*, 212–13.

34 Rebecca Stott, *The Fabrication of the Late Victorian Femme Fatale* (London: Macmillan, 1992), 62, 59.

35 Ibid, 72.

36 Robert Mighall, ' "A pestilence which walketh in darkness": Diagnosing the Victorian Vampire', in Glennis Byron and David

Punter (eds.), *Spectral Readings: Towards a Gothic Geography* (London: Macmillan, 1999), 108–24.

37 'Sub Rosa', *'Dracula', The Gentlewoman*, 21 August 1897, 247.

38 Michel Foucault, *The History of Sexuality: The Will to Knowledge* (London: Penguin, 1998).

39 Regenia Gagnier, 'Evolution and Information or, Eroticism and Everyday life in *Dracula* and Late Victorian Aestheticism', in Regenia Barecca (ed.), *Sex and Death in Victorian Literature* (London: Macmillan, 1990), 144.

40 Stott, *Fabrication of the Late Victorian Femme Fatale*, 84–5.

41 Ibid, 53.

42 David Punter, *The Literature of Terror* (London: Longman, 1996), 425.

43 Stephen Arata, 'The Occidental Tourist: Dracula and the Anxiety of Reverse Colonisation', *Victorian Studies*, 33 (1990), 621–45. The essay also forms part of Arata's later book *Fictions of Loss in the Victorian Fin de Siècle: Identity and Empire* (Cambridge: Cambridge University Press, 1996), 85.

44 See Bill Ashcroft, Gareth Griffiths and Helen Tiffin, *The Empire Writes Back: Theory and Practice in Postcolonial Literatures* (London: 1989). More recently, Ian Duncan has described *Dracula* as an Anglo-Irish novel which 'represents post-famine Ireland in anti-regionalist disguise through the looking glass of Gothic: the land of great hunger is a nation of the undead, sinisterly reorientated to the eastern instead of western limit of Christian Europe'. See 'The Provincial or Regional Novel', in Patrick Brantlinger and William Thesing (eds.), *A Companion to Victorian Fiction* (Oxford: Blackwell, 2002), 328.

45 Cited in Paul Thompson, *The Edwardians* (London: Routledge, 1992), 183.

46 Cosmo Monkhouse, *Punch*, 26 June 1897, 356.

47 Leslie Ann Minot, 'Vamping the Children', 239.

48 Goldsworthy, *Inventing Ruritania, The Imperialism of the Imagination* (London: Yale University Press, 1988), 80–5.

49 Tamar Heller, *Dead Secrets: Wilkie Collins and the Female Gothic* (New Haven: Yale University Press, 1992), 9.

50 Ronald R. Thomas, 'Detection in the Victorian Novel', in Deirdre David (ed.), *The Cambridge Companion to the Victorian Novel*, 182.

51 [Unsigned Review], 'Novels of the Season', *Review of Reviews*, 28 (1903), 638.

52 David Seed, 'Eruptions of the Primitive into the Present: *The Jewel of Seven Stars* and *The Lair of the White Worm*', in Hughes and Smith, *Bram Stoker*, 188.

53 Roger Luckhurst 'Trance-Gothic, 1882–97', in Ruth Robbins and Julian Wolfreys (eds.), *Victorian Gothic: Literary and Cultural Manifestations in the Nineteenth Century* (London: Palgrave, 2000), 163.

54 Richard Pearson 'Archaeology and Gothic Desire: Vitality Beyond the Grave in H. Rider Haggard's Ancient Egypt', in Robbins and Wolfreys, *Victorian Gothic*, 219.

55 Nicholas Daly, 'The Obscure Object of Desire: Victorian Commodity Culture and Fictions of the Mummy', *Novel*, 26 (1994), 44.

56 Ibid, 40.

57 See: Laurence A. Rickels, 'Mummy's Curse', *American Journal of Semiotics*, 9:4 (1992), 47–58.

58 Martin Heidegger, *History of the Concept of Time*, trans. Theodore Kisiel (Bloomington: Indiana University Press, 1985), 150, cited in Julian Wolfreys, *Victorian Hauntings: Spectrality, Gothic, the Uncanny and Literature* (London: Palgrave, 2001), 150.

59 William Barry, 'The Strike of a Sex', *Quarterly Review*, 179 (1894), 294, cited in Richardson, *Women Who Did*, xxxvii.

60 Ruskin, 'Of Queen's Gardens', 73.

61 Lisa Hopkins, 'Crowning the King, Mourning His Mother: *The Jewel of Seven Stars* and *The Lady of the Shroud*', in Hughes and Smith, *Bram Stoker*, 138.

62 Quoted in Sally Ledger, *The New Woman: Fiction and Feminism at the Fin de Siècle* (Manchester: Manchester University Press, 1997), 16.

63 Adriana Craciun, 'Introduction', *Zofloya* (Peterborough: Broadview Press, 1997), 20–1.

64 Rickels, 'Mummy's Curse', 53.

65 Seed, 'Eruptions of the Primitive', 191.

66 Pearson 'Archaeology and Gothic Desire', 236.

CHAPTER 3: MEN AND MONSTERS

1 Robert Louis Stevenson, 'A Gossip About Romance', *Memories and Portraits*, in *The Works of Robert Louis Stevenson* (New York: Charles Scribner's Sons, 1922), XII, 188–9.

2 Lynda Dryden, *Joseph Conrad and the Imperial Romance* (London: Palgrave, 2000). See also: Patrick Brantlinger, *Rule of Darkness: British Literature and Imperialism, 1830–1914* (New York: Cornell University Press, 1993).

3 Deirdre David, 'Empire, Race and the Victorian Novel', in Brantlinger and Thesing, *A Companion to the Victorian Novel*, 96.

4 Dixon, *Writing the Colonial Adventure*, 4.

5 Ibid.

6 Lucy Clifford to Bram Stoker, 15 November 1911, Stoker Collection, Brotherton Library, University of Leeds.

7 [Unsigned Review], '*The Watter's Mou*', *St. James Gazette*, 12 February 1895, 5–6.

8 W. P. Purvis, 'Mr Stoker's New Novel', *Bookman*, 11 February 1909, 98.

9 See Elaine Showalter, *Sexual Anarchy* (London: Bloomsbury, 1992); Harry Brod, 'The New Men's Studies: From Feminist Theory to Gender Scholarship', *Hypatia*, 2 (1987) in J. Kestner, *Masculinities in Victorian Painting* (Aldershot: Ashgate, 1995), 8.

10 Andrew Wynter, *The Borderlands of Insanity* (London: Robert Hardwicke, 1877), 239, 271, 276, in Showalter, *Sexual Anarchy*, 10–11.

11 Quoted in David Trotter, *The English Novel in History 1895–1920*, 146.

12 Dryden, *Joseph Conrad and the Imperial Romance*, 5.

13 Kemp, Mitchell and Trotter, *The Oxford Companion to Edwardian Fiction*, xvi.

14 Glover, *Vampires, Mummies and Liberals*, 48.

15 Ibid, 14.

16 Nicholas Daly, 'Irish Roots: The Romance of History in Bram Stoker's *The Snake's Pass*, *Literature and History*, 4:2 (1995), 62.

17 Luke Gibbons: ' "Some Hysterical Hatred": History, Hysteria and the Literary Revival', *Irish University Review*, 27 (1997), 7–23.

18 In a later essay William Hughes presents a similar view arguing that the bog, 'an overt signal of Irish topography; and the source of derogatory racial stereotypes', is 'an especially rich symbol, one which encodes a reading of Irish problems and British solutions into the fabric of a supposedly local issue.' (18) See ' "For Ireland's Good": The Reconstruction of Rural Ireland in Bram Stoker's *The Snake's Pass*', *Irish Studies Review*, 12 (1995), 17–21.

19 Elizabeth Tilley, 'Stoker, Paris and the Crisis of Identity', *Literature and History*, 10:2 (2001), 33.

20 [Unsigned Review], '*The Snake's Pass*', *Athenaeum*, 20 December 1890, 85.

21 [Unsigned Review], '*The Snake's Pass*', *The Academy*, 3 January 1891, 11.

22 See: Andrew Smith, 'Bram Stoker's *The Mystery of the Sea*: Ireland and the Spanish-Cuban-American War', *Irish Studies Review*, 6:2 (1998), 131–8.

23 Goldsworthy, *Inventing Ruritania*, 8–9.

24 David Stafford, 'Spies and Gentlemen: the birth of the British Spy Novel 1893–1914', *Victorian Studies*, 24 (1981) 489–509, in David Trotter, *The English Novel in History* (London: Routledge, 1993), 169.

25 Glover, *Vampires, Mummies and Liberals*, 14.

26 Goldsworthy, *Inventing Ruritania*, 80.

27 Victor Sage, 'Exchanging Fantasies: Sex and the Serbian Crisis', in Hughes and Smith, *Bram Stoker*, 124.

28 Hughes, *Beyond Dracula*, 101.

29 Lisa Hopkins, 'Crowning the King, Mourning his Mother: *The Jewel of Seven Stars* and *The Lady of the Shroud*', in Hughes and Smith, *Bram Stoker*, 144–5.

30 Hughes, *Beyond Dracula*, 100.

31 Lisa Hopkins, 'Crowning the King', 147.

32 Ibid, 148.

33 Kathleen Blake, *Love and the Woman Question in Victorian Literature* (London, 1983), 82–6.

34 [Unsigned Review], *'The Lair of the White Worm'*, *Times Literary Supplement*, 16 November 1911, 466.

35 Maud Ellman, 'Introduction', *Dracula* (Oxford: Oxford University Press, 1996), x.

36 Oliver Berry, 'Ken Russell', in Yoram Allon, Del Cullen and Hannah Patterson (eds.), *Contemporary British and Irish Film Directors* (London: Wallflower Press, 2001), 299.

37 David Glover, 'Why White?: On Worms and Skin in Bram Stoker's Later Fiction', *Gothic Studies*, 2:3 (2000), 346–60.

38 Lyn Pykett, *The Sensation Novel* (Plymouth: Northcote, 1994), 24.

39 Quoted by George Robb, 'Race Motherhood: Moral Eugenics vs Progressive Eugenics 1880–1920', in Claudia Nelson and Ann Sumner Holmes (eds.), *Maternal Instincts: Visions of Motherhood and Sexuality in Britain 1875–1925* (London: Macmillan, 1997), 63.

40 For a discussion of the novel's interest in mesmerism see David Punter, ' "Echoes in the Animal House": *The Lair of the White Worm'*, in Hughes and Smith, *Bram Stoker*, 173–87.

41 Oliver Lodge to Bram Stoker, 17 November 1911, Stoker Collection, Brotherton Library, University of Leeds.

42 Seed, 'Eruptions of the Primitive into the Present', 201.

CHAPTER 4: WRITING WOMEN

1 Quoted in: George Robb, 'Race Motherhood', 63.

2 [Unsigned Review], *'The Watter's Mou'*, *The Morning Post*, 23 January 1895, 6.

3 [Unsigned Review], *'Miss Betty'*, *North British Review*, 28 February 1898, 2.

4 [Unsigned Review], 'Novel Notes', *The Bookman*, 29 (1905), 38.

5 Jane Gallop, *The Daughter's Seduction* (New York: Cornell University Press, 1982), 77–8.

6 Lyn Pykett, *The Improper Feminine: The Women's Sensation Novel and the New Woman Writing* (London: Routledge, 1992); Sally Ledger, *The New Woman: Fiction and Feminism at the Fin de Siècle* (Manchester: Manchester University Press, 1997); Ann Heilmann, *New Woman Fiction: Women Writing First Wave Feminism* (Basingstoke: Macmillan, 2000).

7 Lynda Nead, *Myths of Sexuality*, (Oxford: Blackwells, 1988), 91.

8 Lyn Pykett, *The Sensation Novel*, 45.

9 Clement Scott *Pall Mall Gazette*, 8 April 1891. Cited in Jean Chothia (ed.), *The New Woman* (Oxford: Oxford University Press, 1998), i.

10 [Unsigned Review], *'The Fate of Fenella'*, *The Bookseller*, 3 June 1892, 518; [Unsigned Review]. *'The Fate of Fenella'*, *The Academy*, 23 July 1892, 68.

11 Lillian Nayder, 'Decadent Detection: *The Fate of Fenella*' (1891–92) and Mystery for Mystery's Sake' (unpublished paper delivered at the Victorians Institute Conference, 1999), 4. I am very grateful to Professor Nayder for making available a copy of her paper.

12 [Unsigned Review], *'Miss Betty'*, *The Bookman*, April 1898, 21.

13 [Unsigned Review], *'Miss Betty'*, *North British Daily Review*, 28 February 1898, 2.

14 Len Platt, *Aristocracies of Fiction* (London: Greenwood, 2001), 30.

15 [Unsigned Review], *'Miss Betty'*, *The Speaker*, 5 March 1898, 306.

16 Jameson, *The Political Unconscious*.

17 [Unsigned Review], 'Some New Novels', *St. James Budget*, 22 February 1895, 22.

18 Alison Light, ' "Young Bess": Historical Novels and Growing Up', *Feminist Review*, 33 (1988), 66.

19 Jeffrey Weeks, *Sex Politics and Society: The Regulation of Sexuality Since 1800* (London: Longman, 1981), 25.

20 Simone De Beauvoir, *The Second Sex* (1949), in Ruth Robbins, ' "Snowed Up": Feminist Perspectives', in Wolfreys and Baker, *Literary Theories*, 118.

21 Heilmann, *New Woman Fiction*, 51.

22 [Unsigned Review], *'The Man'*, *The Bookman*, October 1905, 38.

23 Alys W. Pearsall Smith, 'A Reply from the Daughters', *Nineteenth Century*, 35 (1894), 443, in Heilmann, *New Woman Fiction*, 40.

24 Quoted in George Robb, 'Race Motherhood', 63.

25 See Heilmann, *New Woman Fiction*, 170.

26 Barbara Creed, 'Kristeva, Femininity, Abjection', in Ken Gelder (ed.), *The Horror Reader* (London: Routledge, 2000), 64.

27 [Unsigned Review], 'Novel Notes', *The Bookman*, August 1897, 29.

28 Lillian Nayder, 'Virgin Territory and the Iron Virgin: Engendering the Empire in Bram Stoker's "The Squaw" ', in Nelson and Holmes, *Maternal Instincts*, 77.

29 Eric Sundquist, *Home As Found: Authority and Genealogy in Nineteenth Century American Literature* (Baltimore: Johns Hopkins University Press, 1979), 91.

30 Nayder, 'Virgin Territory', 84.

31 Nayder, 'Virgin Territory', 109–10, 90.

32 Jane Gallop, 'Keys to Dora', in *In Dora's Case: Freud – Hysteria – Feminism*, ed. Charles Bernheimer and Claire Kahane (New York: Virago, 1985), 209.

33 Carolyn Dever, *Death and the Mother: From Dickens to Freud* (London: Macmillan, 1998), 109.

34 Jim Reilly in *Shadowtime* (London: Routledge, 1993) uses this term to designate the female figure 'who wields the phallic tools of the symbolic order, of language and culture....', 89.

35 Nayder, 'Virgin Territory', 84–5.

36 Claire Stewart, '"Weird Fascination": The Response to Victorian Women's Ghost Stories', in Emma Liggins and Daniel Duffy (eds.), *Feminist Readings of Victorian Popular Texts* (Aldershot: 2001), 114.

37 Diana Basham, *The Trial of Woman: Feminism and the Occult Sciences in Victorian Literature and Society* (London: Macmillan, 1992), 158.

38 Nickianne Moody, 'Visible Margins: Women Writers and the Ghost Story', in Sarah Seats and Gail Cunningham (eds.), *Image and Power: Women in Fiction in the Twentieth Century* (London: Longman, 1996), 77.

39 Mark Wigley, *The Architecture of Deconstruction: Derrida's Haunt* (1993), 108, in Julian Wolfreys, *Victorian Hauntings: Spectrality, Gothic, the Uncanny and Literature* (London: Palgrave, 2001), 111.

40 T. H. Huxley, *Evolution and Ethics* (London: Macmillan, 1894), 12.

41 Marion Shaw, 'Elizabeth Gaskell, Tennyson and the Fatal Return: Sylvia's Lovers and Enoch Arden', *Gaskell Society Journal*, 9 (1995), 47.

42 See Shaw, Ibid, for a further discussion of this trope.

43 Eve Kosofsky Sedgwick, *Between Men: English Literature and Male Homosocial Desire* (New York: Columbia University Press, 1993).

44 Cited in Alan Sinfield, *Literature, Politics and Culture in Post-war Britain* (Oxford: Blackwell, 1989), 25.

Select Bibliography

WORKS BY BRAM STOKER

Where applicable, the dates given are those of the first English editions of the works in book form.

Novels and Novellas

'The Primrose Path: A Serial in Ten Chapters', *The Shamrock*, 12 (1875), 289–93, 312–17, 330–4, 345–9, 360–5.

'Buried Treasures: A Serial in Four Chapters', *The Shamrock*, 12 (1875), 376–9, 403–6.

The Duties of Clerks of Petty Sessions in Ireland (Dublin: Falconer, 1879).

Under the Sunset (London: Sampson, Low & Co., 1882).

A Glimpse of America (London: Sampson, Low & Co., 1886).

The Snake's Pass (London: Sampson, Low & Co., 1890).

The Fate of Fenella, A novel by 24 authors, 3 Vols (London: Hutchinson and Co., 1892).

The Watter's Mou (London: A. Constable & Co., The Acme Library, 1895).

The Shoulder of Shasta (London: A. Constable & Co., 1895).

Dracula (London: A. Constable & Co., 1897).

Miss Betty (London: C. Arthur Pearson, 1898).

The Mystery of the Sea (London: William Heinemann, 1902).

The Jewel of Seven Stars (London: William Heinemann, 1903).

The Man (London: William Heinemann, 1905).

Personal Reminisences of Henry Irving, 2 Vols (London: William Heinemann, 1906).

Lady Athlyne (London: William Heinemann, 1908).

'The Censorship of Fiction', *The Nineteenth Century and After*, 64 (September 1908), 479–87.

Snowbound: The Record of a Theatrical Touring Party (London: Collier, 1908).

The Lady of the Shroud (London: William Heinemann, 1909).

Famous Imposters (London: Sidgwick and Jackson, 1910).

The Lair of the White Worm (London: William Rider, 1911).

Dracula's Guest and Other Weird Stories (London: George Routledge, 1914).

BIOGRAPHY

There are numerous accounts of Stoker's life. The most detailed are:

Belford, Barbara, *Bram Stoker: His Life and Times* (London: Weidenfeld & Nicolson, 1996). Psychobiography that focuses largely on the formative influences of Stoker's early life and his relationship with Irving.

Caine, Hall, 'Bram Stoker: The Story of a Great Friendship', *Daily Telegraph*, 24 April 1912, 16. A partial (in both senses of the word) account of Stoker written by one of his best friends but useful for the light it sheds on how Stoker's contemporaries saw him.

Farson, Daniel, *The Man Who Wrote Dracula: A Biography of Bram Stoker* (London: Joseph, 1975). A contentious account of Stoker's life, which gained notoriety for the theories it put forward as to the cause of Stoker's death.

Ludlam, Harry, *A Biography of Dracula: The Life Story of Bram Stoker* (London: Foulsham, 1962). For many years the standard life of Stoker, completed with the approval of his son, Noel.

Osborough, W. N., 'The Dublin Castle Career (1866–78) of Bram Stoker', *Gothic Studies*, 1:2 (December 1999), 222–40.

Pozzuoli, Alain, *Bram Stoker: Prince des Ténèbres* (Paris: Librarie Seguier, 1989).

CRITICAL WORKS

The amount of critical literature on Stoker (most of it devoted to *Dracula*) is considerable. For a more extensive bibliography see William Hughes, *Bram Stoker (Abraham Stoker) 1847–1912: A Bibliography* (Queensland: University of Queensland, Victorian Fiction Research Guides, 1997).

Arata, Stephen D., 'The Occidental Tourist', *Victorian Studies*, 33 (1990), 621–45). Arata considers the novel in the light of late nineteenth-century feelings of fear about the colonization of England by primitive forces. Arata continues the argument in his *Fictions of Loss in the Victorian Fin de Siècle: Identity and Empire* (Cambridge: Cambridge University Press, 1996).

158

Auerbach, Nina, *Our Vampires, Ourselves* (Chicago: University of Chicago Press, 1995). Discusses the history of vampires and the different meanings they hold for successive generations.

Baldick, Chris, Robert Mighall, 'Gothic Criticism' in David Punter (ed.), *A Companion to the Gothic* (Oxford: Blackwell, 2000), 209–28. An essay that takes issue with the critical predisposition to describe *fin de siècle* Gothic writing as statements of 'anxiety.'

Byron, Glennis (ed.), *Dracula (New Casebooks)*, (London: Macmillan, 1998). An anthology of influential theoretically-informed essays on Stoker's most famous novel.

Carter, Margaret L. (ed.), *Dracula: The Vampire and the Critics* (Ann Arbor: UMI Research Press, 1988). Collection of essays on Stoker's most famous novel, useful for revealing the different (sometimes bizarre) frameworks within which critics have attempted to read it.

Case, Alison A., *Plotting Women: Gender and Narration in the Eighteenth and Nineteenth Century British Novel* (London: University Press of Virginia, 1999). Helpful discussion of the different narrative strands of *Dracula*, with the emphasis on Mina Harker as storyteller.

Craft, Christopher, ' "Kiss Me with Those Red Lips": Gender and Inversion in Bram Stoker's *Dracula*', *Representations,* 8 (1984), 107–33. Enormously influential essay that situates the novel within *fin de siècle* anxieties about the instability of gender roles and interrogates its homosexual sub-text.

Daly, Nicholas, *Modernism, Romance, and the Fin de Siècle: Popular Fiction and British Culture, 1880–1914* (Cambridge: Cambridge University Press, 2000). Situates Stoker within the context of the 'romance revival', the new imperialism and the rise of professionalism, but suggests too that his adventure, vampire and mummy novels look forward to modernist developments. Includes discussions of *The Snake's Pass, Dracula* and *The Jewel of Seven Stars*.

Deane, Seamus, *Strange Country: Modernity and Nationhood in Irish Writing Since 1790* (Oxford: Clarendon Press, 1997). One of the few works to consider Stoker as an Irish writer who interrogates contemporary Irish issues: 'Dracula's dwindling soil and his vampiric appetites consort well enough with the image of the Irish landlord current in the nineteenth century. Running out of soil, this peculiar version of the absentee landlord in London will flee the light of day and be consigned to the only territory left to him, that of legend.'

Gagnier, Regenia, 'Evolution and Information: or, Eroticism and Everyday Life, in Dracula and Late Victorian Aestheticism', in Regina Barreca (ed.), *Sex and Death in Victorian Literature* (Bloomington: Indiana University Press, 1989), 140–57.

Garnett, Rhys, '*Dracula* and *The Beetle*: Imperial and Sexual Guilt and Fear in Late Victorian Fantasy', in R.J. Ellis and Rhys Garnett (eds.), *Science Fiction Roots and Branches* (London: Macmillan, 1990), 30–55.

Gelder, Ken, *Reading the Vampire* (London: Routledge, 1994). Wide-ranging discussion of the figure of the vampire, its cultural contexts and meanings and changing manifestations in fiction, television and cinema.

Glover, David, *Vampires, Mummies and Liberals: Bram Stoker and the Politics of Popular Fiction* (London: Duke University Press, 1996). Important and detailed analysis of the cultural contexts of Stoker's novels, which reads the novels as metaphorical condensations of specific anxieties faced by the Victorian middle classes in the 1890s, a decade when 'the high point of the Victorian era was now past and the signs of decadence were plainly visible for anyone to see'. Stoker is a writer in crisis. Includes readings of *The Snake's Pass*, *Lady Athlyne*, *The Man*, *Dracula*, *The Lair of the White Worm*.

———'Why White?: On Worms and Skin in Bram Stoker's Later Fiction', *Gothic Studies*, 2 (December 2000), 346–360. Excellent discussion of *The Lair of the White Worm* and its contexts.

Griffin, Gale B., ' "Your girls that you love are mine": *Dracula* and the Victorian Male Sexual Imagination', *International Journal of Women's Studies*, 3 (1980), 454–65.

Halberstam, Judith, 'Technologies of Monstrosity: Bram Stoker's *Dracula*', *Victorian Studies*, 3:3 (1993), 333–52.

Heffernan, James A., 'Looking at the Monster', *Critical Inquiry*, 24 (1997), 133–58. Discusses film versions of *Dracula*.

Hughes, William, *Beyond Dracula: Bram Stoker's Fiction and its Cultural Contexts* (London: Macmillan, 2000). A detailed historicist analysis, which sees in Stoker's novels the multiplicity of late Victorian and Edwardian experiences as they relate to discourses of gender, theology, nationhood and medicine. Includes readings of *Under the Sunset*, *Dracula*, *The Man* and *The Mystery of the Sea*.

——— and Andrew Smith, *Bram Stoker: History, Psychoanalysis and the Gothic* (London: Macmillan, 1998). An important series of essays designed to contest 'the orthodoxy...which contends that Bram Stoker was the author of only one work of note'.

Ledger, Sally, *The New Woman: Fiction and Feminism at the Fin de Siècle* (Manchester: Manchester University Press, 1997). A wide-ranging analysis of the 'Woman Question' which locates *Dracula* within the cultural context of sexual decadence and imperialism.

Macfie, Sian, ' "They Suck Us Dry": A Study of Late Nineteenth Century Projections of Vampiric Women', in Philip Shaw and Peter Stockwell (eds.), *Subjectivity and Literature from the Romantics to the Present Day* (London: Pinter, 1991), 58–67. Situates Stoker's vampire in the literary context of the 1890s.

Malchow, Howard L., *Gothic Images of Race in Nineteenth Century Britain* (Stanford: Stanford University Press, 1996). A challenging reading of Stoker and *Dracula*, which locates Stoker's novel against the backdrop of contemporary anxieties inspired by homosexuals, Jack the Ripper killings and the apparently threatening presence of Jewish immigrants. *Dracula* is an anti-Semitic novel concerned with the need to save Britain from the threats embodied in a racial 'other'.

Mighall, Robert, *Geography of Victorian Gothic: Mapping History's Nightmares* (Oxford: Oxford University Press, 1999). Historically-based analysis of different manifestations of Gothic writing in *Dracula* and in contemporaries like Robert Louis Stevenson.

Moretti, Franco, *Signs Taken for Wonders: Essays in the Sociology of Literary Forms*. Trans. Susan Fischer, David Forgacs, and David Miller (London: Verso, 1983), 83–108. Much-quoted Marxist reading of *Dracula*, influential in the gradual move towards more historicist readings of the novel.

Nayder, Lillian, 'Virgin Territory and the Iron Virgin: Engendering the Empire in Bram Stoker's "The Squaw"'. In Claudia Nelson and Ann Sumner Holmes (eds.), *Maternal Instincts: Visions of Motherhood and Sexuality in Britain 1875–1925* (London: Macmillan, 1995). A penetrating analysis of this short story, which considers the ways in which a range of imperial, sexual and maternal anxieties infiltrate the narrative.

Pick, Daniel, 'Terrors of the Night': *Dracula* and "Degeneration" in the Late Nineteenth Century', *Critical Quarterly*, 30 (1988), 71–87. A very accessible discussion of the ways in which contemporary visions of degeneration infiltrate *Dracula* and *The Man*.

Richardson, Maurice, 'The Psychoanalysis of Ghost Stories', *Twentieth Century*, 166 (1959), 419–31. Groundbreaking early analysis of *Dracula* that argues that the novel is 'a quite blatant demonstration of the Oedipus complex. The attempts by the male characters to defeat the Count represent attempts to destroy the sexually overpowering father.

Rickels, Laurence A., 'Mummy's Curse', *American Journal of Semiotics*, 9 (1992), 47–58. Insightful and witty analysis of *The Jewel of Seven Stars*.

Robbins, Ruth, *Pater to Forster, 1873–1924* (London: Palgrave, 2003). A useful general overview, which situates Stoker alongside other writers and literary developments of the period.

Roth, Phyllis, *Bram Stoker* (Boston: Twayne, 1982). An important early study of Stoker's novels, informed by the tenets of feminism and psychoanalysis.

Schaffer, Talia, ' "A Wilde Desire Took me": The Homoerotic History of

Dracula', *ELH*, 61:2 (1994), 381–426.

Seed, David, 'The Narrative Method of Dracula', *Nineteenth Century Fiction*, 40 (1985), 33–49.

Senf, Carol A., (ed.), *The Critical Response to Bram Stoker* (Westport: Greenwood Press, 1994). A collection of critical responses to the works from the early reviews to assessments in the late 1980s.

——— *Dracula: Between Tradition and Modernism* (Boston: Twayne, 1998). Useful summary of the varied ways in which this novel can be read.

Skal, David, *Hollywood Gothic: The Tangled Web of Dracula From Novel to Stage to Screen* (London: Andre Deutsch, 1992). Examines well-known film adaptations of *Dracula*.

Smith, Andrew and Hughes, William (eds.), *Empire and the Gothic* (London: Palgrave, 2002). Series of post-colonial readings of Gothic texts, including *Dracula*.

Spencer, Kathleen, 'Purity and Danger: *Dracula*, the Urban Gothic, and the Late Victorian Degeneracy Crisis', *ELH*, 59:1 (1992), 197–225.

Stott, Rebecca, *The Fabrication of the Late Victorian Femme Fatale* (London: Macmillan, 1992). A historicist reading of the novels which relates the depiction of race and gender relations in *Dracula* and *The Lair of the White Worm* to much wider contemporary fears about the need to 'patrol' and maintain the health of the nation.

Tilley, Elizabeth, 'Stoker, Paris and the Crisis of Identity', *Literature and History*, 10:2 (2001), 26–41. A detailed analysis of the short story 'The Crisis of the Rats.'

Valente, Joseph, *Dracula's Crypt: Bram Stoker, Irishness and the Question of Blood* (Urbana: University of Illinois Press, 2002). An account that underlines a good deal of what has already been noted but not fully explored, that is the extent of Stoker's awkward relationship with Irish politics. Includes readings of *The Primrose Path, Dracula*, and the short story 'The Dualitists'.

Wicke, Jennifer, 'Vampiric Typewriting: Dracula and its Media', *ELH*, 59 (1992), 467–93. An influential essay dealing with the connections between technology, vampirism and mass culture in Stoker's most famous novel.

Index